The Excellency of the Word

The George Craig Stewart Memorial Lectures in Preaching

THE EXCELLENCY
OF THE WORD

by
WILLIAM H. NES

Professor of Homiletics
Seabury-Western Theological Seminary
Evanston, Illinois.

Together with
A Survey of Homiletics Education

by
NOAH E. FEHL

Assistant Professor of the History and Philosophy
of Religion
Seabury-Western Theological Seminary.

MOREHOUSE-GORHAM CO.
NEW YORK

The Scripture quotations in this book designated *R.S.V.*
are from the Revised Standard Version of *The Holy
Bible*, copyrighted 1946 and 1952 by the Division of
Christian Education, National Council of Churches.

Contents

The Excellency of the Word

Lecture 1

THE PREACHER AND THE BIBLE

IN THE Office of Institution, as you will remember, there is a prayer of the new incumbent in which he implores the grace of God in all the duties of his ministry. For his preaching, he asks for "a readiness of thought and expression suitable to the clearness and excellency of thy holy Word." But before this he has prayed that God will fill his memory with the words of His Law and will enlighten his understanding with the illumination of the Holy Ghost. The Christian pulpit is not for the display of eloquence or intellect, but being the vehicle of embassy, it is charged with a message and with the business of negotiating the reconciliation of man to God. As in the case of any serious embassage its work will be performed best with eloquence and intellect provided it be animated by wisdom and fidelity. In one who speaks and acts for a superior, therefore, it is required that he make his master's business his own and that he seek to discharge it with the greatest skill to which he can attain. If the minds of men are to be informed with Christian doctrine, the preacher must first understand it himself—and who can understand it that has not grappled earnestly and honestly with its problems?—and then he must find ways of making it intelligible to his hearers, for, as St. Augustine says in a book to which I shall frequently allude, until a man understand you, you haven't spoken to him at all. Furthermore, if hearts are to be opened to God's love and made favorable to receiving His Gospel, the words of its delivery must be suitable to the marvellous interfusion of its sweetness and its severity. But since, in the loftiest sense, the preaching of the Gospel and the teaching of the Faith are uncompromisingly pragmatic in their purpose, and demand always a response of action, however interior it may be, there is a persuasion to be accomplished, a commitment to ensue, which must evoke from the preacher a noble eloquence, sometimes of solemn rebuke, sometimes of passionate entreaty, and always filled and reverberating, like a canyon through which a mighty river flows, with the majesty and love of God.

To speak in a manner suitable to the clearness and excellency of the Divine Word, is to speak intelligibly, artistically, and movingly; and since in saying this I am echoing St. Augustine, I should like at this point to say something of Book 4 of his *De Doctrina Christiana*. A man naturally wishes to commend to his friends a book which has profoundly impressed his own mind, and if it be classical to the Christian inheritance, I think he may be the more indulged in doing so. It is the first Christian treatise on homiletics and I have been astonished at its absence from a number of homiletical bibliographies which I have seen, as though someone were to compile a corpus of American documents omitting the Declaration of Independence. Even the analogy is not too fantastic because incidental to what else he has to say is a manifesto of freedom from the sterility into which the classical tradition of oratory had fallen. In this sense it is true, as Archbishop Brilioth has said, that "Augustine has striven to free the sermon from its bondage to an alien tradition." [1] Yet Cicero is to him still the master of rhetoric and

[1] *Landmarks in the History of Preaching*, by Ynge Brilioth. S.P.C.K., 1950.

13

the authority for its determinative principles, *docere*, *delectare*, and *movere;* and as well for the *genera dicendi, tenue, temperatum,* and *grande:* to speak of small matters in a subdued manner, of moderately important matters in a measured manner, and of great things in a majestic manner. The measure of its continuity and discontinuity with the tradition of Greek and Roman oratory no less than the historical significance for Christianity of this work of Augustine has been succinctly stated by Professor Charles Sears Baldwin:

> With this elaborate pedagogical tradition [the Sophistic], a sharp break is made by St. Augustine. The fourth book of his De Doctrina Christiana has historical significance in the early years of the fifth century out of all proportion to its size; for it begins rhetoric anew. It not only ignores sophistic; it goes back over centuries of the lore of personal triumph to the ancient idea of moving men to truth; and it gives to the vital counsels of Cicero a new emphasis for the urgent tasks of preaching the word of God.[2]

This is what Augustine has to say: Truth needs eloquence if it is to be effectively communicated,

[2] *Medieval Rhetoric and Poetry*, by Charles Sears Baldwin. Macmillan, 1928. Chapter 2.

and eloquence grows more from reading and listening than from rules. Yet an eloquence acquired by this vital imitation will be found to conform to the canons of literary taste and the rules formulated by Cicero just as children brought up among those who speak correctly will recognize faulty speech when they hear it and will themselves speak properly. There is an eloquence in Holy Scripture and a literary excellence for which Christians have no reason to be ashamed; and this is true also with regard to the writers and preachers most esteemed by the Church. Here is a double answer both to pagan critics and to those Christians who, affecting to despise all worldly eloquence, refuse instruction on what and how to teach because, as they say, the Holy Ghost makes them teachers; for both alike are blind to the majesty of Scripture and to the noble propriety of its style because they imagine that an inflated and ostentatious style is all that eloquence consists in. Those who rely solely on inspiration might as well decline to pray because our Lord says, "Your Father knoweth what things ye have need of before you ask Him." The Christian orator, then, who transmits Christ to his disciples must himself be filled with that which he is about to distribute; but must also do what he can to be heard with intelligence, with pleasure, and with obedience. "And who can make us say what we ought, and in the way we ought, except He in whose hand both we and our speeches are?" There can therefore be no question about the need for prayer, and since there can be more than one good way of saying a thing, one should pray for divine guidance before he opens his mouth to teach others. But when it is understood that the aids of teaching through human agency are spiritually efficacious only when God works through them, it is evident that the Christian orator will not despise these aids or be careless in using them. In exposition he must strive for clarity, since you have not spoken to a man really until he has understood you. Moreover, since in teaching he must often expose error or resolve doubt, he must first understand what he says and must never stoop to wrangling or disingenuous argument nor yet seek to be applauded for his own keenness of intellect. And again, in trying to move his hearers to the love of the truth, he will avoid a profuse and showy style; he will, nevertheless, use ornament with propriety, as for example figures of speech and the balance and rhythm which have already been remarked in Holy Scripture. But above all, he seeks to move men to obey what they have been led to understand and moved to love. For this we cannot do better than to consider the modes of speaking, to observe their use by some of our most eminent preachers, such as St. Ambrose and St. Cyprian, and to employ them with skill and sincerity. There is a time and place for quiet reasonableness, and for imaginative expression in the beauty of language, and for solemn admonition or passionate entreaty; and even in the same sermon, if for no better reason than to avoid wearying the hearers, these may alternate and blend one with another; but at the last it is the sublime eloquence of deep emotion that can alone prevail upon insensitivity to duty. But only a man who is good and wise can do this, for people will cease to listen to a man who does not listen to himself, no matter how eloquent he may be; and from learning to despise the preacher they will go on to despise the Word of God.

Now this has been a very imperfect abstract of a very great document, and you can no more get from it what St. Augustine really has to say than you can walk across a river on the mechanical drawing of a bridge. Yet I hope that it may lead you to walk across a noble span built long ago but still standing sturdily, and indeed safer and pleasanter to tread than many that are later and lighter. Perhaps I may have suggested to you something of the deep Christian integrity and simple common sense of this treatise. It reads well, even aloud. At all events, if a man reads any books on preaching, he ought to read this, for he will find in it much to think upon.

It has a great deal to say about the preacher's dependence on Scripture, and assumes that Scripture is familiar to Church people. The declared purpose of the whole work is to afford guidance on Christian instruction, the first three books dealing with what is to be taught, and the fourth with how to teach it. That Augustine considered it a matter of great importance is evident from the interval between its being begun and being completed: for in 397 he had written as far as Chapter 25 of Book III, and the rest of it was not written until nearly thirty years later, and then at the cost of some interruption to his preoccupying work on the *Retractations*. Speaking of the dissatisfaction an author is likely to feel even when he has closed his book, a certain writer has said, "One does not finish a work; one abandons it." If ever a man would let a thing go, unless he felt a deep compulsion to carry it forward, it would be after such a time of abandonment. In his account of how he came to this, he says he finished the whole work in four books, "the first three affording aids to the interpretation of Scripture, the last giving directions as to the mode of making known our interpretation." Now this is quite plain as it describes the contents of the book, and the plan of its composition. But in this alone it is a matter of interest only to the commentator upon Augustine or to the Church historian. What is of much deeper significance is the manner in which Holy Scripture is conceived as controlling the mind of the preacher and the substance of his sermon.

Does this bring us to what is often called "Bible preaching"? Yes, it does, if you are thinking by contrast of certain kinds of preaching related scarcely at all or only casually to Scripture. It is difficult to be specific in example without caricaturing what one disapproves; and since most preachers have little opportunity to hear others, their own sermons will be their most extensive source material for finding fault with contemporary preaching. That, of course, is why the giving of these lectures is such a disturbing adventure: it brings me to so many backward and inward glances. While for you there is not yet so much behind you for judicious condemnation, you can determine within yourselves, in the illumination of your studies here, what is the right kind of preaching. Of course you must be conformed to God's will, for otherwise your words will not be; of course you must be in grace, for otherwise you will not go forth with grace; of course you must have the right to stand in God's house, for otherwise you will have none to stand in His pulpit. These are the greatest things, but we are not now speaking of them. The essential thing about right preaching, as we are thinking of it now, is the orbit in which it moves, the source from which its matter is taken, the authority for what it speaks. The Sovereign *for* whom you speak and the Authority *by* whom you speak is the Triune God. But since you point me to this Authority, where is the Testimony by which I can know that your words are His Word?

Now if St. Augustine had been a Protestant, you might properly regard this book of his as a manifesto for the Bible and the Bible only as the religion of Protestants. And you might the more be disposed to think so when you find him using the phrase, "the rule of faith," with reference not to the Creed, but rather to the Summary of the Law. But he was a Catholic. To be sure, he was a Catholic of his day, of the patristic Church. Then, as Duchesne has said, "The Papacy, such as the West knew it later on, was still to be born," [3] though Innocent I was diligent in hastening its birth. In the Church then, notwithstanding the vehemence of its controversies and with full allowance for its own legacy of conflict for the future, there were the clear possibilities of a Catholic development out of which the present disastrous confusion and disunity of Christendom need not have ensued. In particular, the later controversies about the relation of Scripture and tradition were not inevitable, and it is from these that the present confusion of Christianity to a very large extent arises.

[3] *The Early History of the Church*, by Mgr. Louis Duchesne. English ed., Longmans. Vol. II, p. 522.

For before us is a book written by a Catholic Father in which Holy Scripture is presumed to validate the tradition of the Church because it is presumed to determine that tradition, in all essential matters. To interpret Scripture must be the preacher's business because the Church is the interpreter of Scripture. If the preacher falls into heresy his interpretation must be refuted by the better and wiser interpretation of the Church. This is commonplace both in the Fathers and in the Councils. If the unity of the Church is to be preserved, which is at its root the unity of charity, false teaching must be opposed; if possible, it must be corrected; and when this fails, it must be condemned and forbidden by competent authority. You will see this in the New Testament. And the same thing is true of moral error, for neither with regard to belief nor yet with regard to conduct is the Church a society of anarchists. Christianity is not a merchant ship sailing the flux of time; rather it is a lightship anchored to one historic moment, and the anchor that holds it is the Canon of Scripture. If this were not so there would have been little occasion for so much endeavor to fix the content and limits of the Canon. To hold that the Scriptures contain all things necessary for Christian faith has its difficulties, no doubt, but it does not undermine either the authority or the responsibility of the Church "in controversies of faith." But to hold that Scripture and tradition are co-ordinate authorities betrays an anxiety about the truth of the tradition which the early Church did not suffer, and it brings in its train certain results which have proved to be catastrophic.

How can anyone discerningly read the Gospels without perceiving that it was this kind of dichotomy, this uncontrolled accretion of tradition which inevitably becomes an incubus, that was at the center of our Lord's conflict with the Pharisees? In the Church, the same kind of thing has led with a certain irresistible momentum to the conclusion that what the Church comes to believe, provided it be formulated and approved by ecclesiastical authority, can rise to the position of dogma without necessary reference to Scripture or demonstrable ground in ancient tradition. There lurks behind this something substantially Montanist, to the extent at any rate of postulating a dispensation of the Holy Spirit for the revelation of a fuller Gospel rather than, as the Church is bound to hold, for the fuller illumination of the Gospel. When, therefore, alleged tradition is found to be an accumulation of novelties often in direct contradiction to ancient tradition, it forfeits its right to that very authority that genuine tradition can properly command. All this does not go unnoticed or unchallenged, but only by a few, and here and there, until some flaming crisis comes when all the unregarded pressures, all the frustrations of the reforming spirit, and all the grievances of masses of people break forth, focused, as in the sixteenth century, primarily in a single man, with the appalling denouement that the disintegration of Christian community becomes a scandal in the world for centuries. From this distance and in many slanting historical lights, we may somewhat doubt whether the rediscovery of the Bible was as completely a rediscovery, or that behind it the ignorance had been as dismal, as Protestants widely have supposed. But *then* they thought so. The light of Scripture had broken like a fiery and splendid dawn upon a decadent Church and brought escape from the darkness of evils entrenched in ecclesiastical tradition. On the Continent neither side mistook the position of the other. The Council of Trent, in Session iv, declares that it "receives and venerates with an equal feeling of piety and reverence all the books of the Old and New Testament . . . and also the traditions relating as well to faith as to morals. . . ." The Protestant reaction was so to exalt Holy Scripture as to deprive Catholic tradition of any force whatever. In the calamitous sequel the one side has moved forward to a dogma that rests neither on any clear testimony of Holy Scripture nor on the genuinely continuous tradition of the Church, while a further dogma seems to be in the making by which access to Christ would depend upon the intercession of His mother, *ad Jesum per Mariam;* and the other side has as inexorably moved through four hundred years of efflorescent sectarianism and doctrinal confusion to a place where, now that the evil of this is growing plainer, the principles of reintegration are hidden in the confusion which submerged them.

I have not spoken of the Anglican Church. It was deeply involved in the Reformation and has continuously felt within itself, and manifested unmistakably, the characteristics of that movement in ways that have been neither all good nor all bad. But as Clement Webb remarked, one of its most notable characteristics, and this notwithstanding its world-wide diffusion, has been insularity.[4] On the crucial matter of Scripture and tradition it holds neither the Roman nor the Protestant position.[5] For a century past it has in many things taken its current colors both from surrounding Protestantism and Roman Catholicism according to the differing

[4] *A Century of Anglican Theology*, by Clement C. J. Webb. Morehouse-Gorham Co.

[5] This is true also of the Orthodox Church; for while it commonly speaks of the relation of Scripture and tradition in a manner apparently indistinguishable from the statement of Trent, it is speaking nevertheless of tradition in a far more static sense; that is to say, as being the patristic tradition and the Decrees of the seven Ecumenical Councils. In the Encyclical of the Church of Constantinople dated August, 1895, this is given its widest extension to mean what the Eastern and Western Churches "unanimously professed before the ninth century." For the authenticity and authority of tradition this is an "appeal to antiquity" no less emphatic than that of classical Anglicanism. This, of course, lies open to the charge of the "archaic fallacy": for the ancient Church was far from being static; and development—which is apparent in the New Testament itself—cannot be artificially punctuated with a period. Yet in any theory of development, what is always at stake is the peculiar, the unique, the definitive authority of Holy Scripture in its control and judgment upon all development. Moreover, since by the very dynamics of history, and of Christianity itself, development was as inevitable as it has been actual, there is the more need of such a control. By whatever "living voice" the Church speaks—and this certainly applies to the preacher—the voice must be the voice of the Gospel in the New Testament.

predilections of its ecclesiastical parties. Its scholarship has been better than its preaching, and, at least in this country, it has not had the kind of missionary zeal, except here and there, to spur any serious endeavor to become a Church for the populace. It has in its safe deposit box some tremendous assets (and I don't mean money, for that is in the boxes of its members but not to any commensurate extent in its own)—some tremendous assets, I repeat, that could have been and yet may be of inestimable use to the Christian world. I hope, gentlemen, that you will see to it, for in this, as in so much else, you must be better than your fathers.

You cannot meet this challenge unless you are, in the highest sense of the words, Scripture preachers. This will require of you a constant study of the Bible, a veritable immersion in it. It will require of you an irreproachable integrity in handling it. It will force you to face and deeply ponder some very serious questions and under no temptation from fear or ignorance to evade them. What effect, for example, has a century of intensive criticism had on the authority, the interpretation, and the use of Scripture? What new orientation of Christian thought must be made to the indisputably vast backward sweep of human history, to the immense accumulation of knowledge about the religions of mankind, or to the irrefutable involvement of man in the organic evolution and interrelation of all living creatures on this planet? In the whole field of human knowledge, as in technics, there has taken place since the end of the eighteenth century a revolution that stands among the few most determinative in human history. Between six and eight thousand years ago man passed, perhaps with a similarly startling irruption of new knowledge and inventiveness, from a food-gathering to an agricultural society; now he has passed to an industrial society where even his agriculture takes on, as it must, the character of a thoroughly scientific operation. Now is all this the work of the Devil? I have heard from many mouths and read in many books in my own lifetime that it is. I have been told that the Christian Faith lies in total jeopardy because of it. But I do not believe this. I remain convinced that the acquisition of knowledge is not an affront to God and that truth of fact is to be accepted as a duty to that Divine Reason which has so made the universe that the fact is there. Whether he has much knowledge or little, few implements or many, the tragedy of man is not his knowledge or his technics but his denial of his creaturehood, his idolatry of what he makes and of himself, and his murderous inhumanity.

So do not, I beg you, be frightened of natural or historical science, or of the enquiring and critical spirit as it applies its methods of research into the Bible or Christian institutions or the nature and phenomena of religion. Do you propose to abandon these to the opponents of the Faith? If, as Augustine said of rhetoric, they can use them, so can you, and to a better purpose. The findings of the new knowledge are by no means all in, and the "assured results" not in all matters "assured." Yet there is, if one may put it so, a new shape of knowledge with color and contour different from that of our ancestors. But what is of even greater significance is the quality of scrupulous fidelity to fact that animates genuine scientific inquiry in any field. Ah yes, I have often heard it said, this is precisely where the trouble lies, that is to say, in indifference to "value." On the contrary, that is precisely where its virtue lies, and where its limitation is: for at the level of fact the inquiry must be detached; and although there is in this, it is true, an epistemological problem, I submit to you that if there is a discrepancy in the Gospels with regard to the date of the Crucifixion, you cannot say that you will not admit this if it raises for you a question concerning the inspiration of Scripture. I can think of nothing that will better please the real Enemy than to let him have the monopoly of objective truth. You must not carry such a poisonous infection to your people.

But this is being done by a certain kind of Bible preaching very widely prevalent and held in some quarters to be the only pure Bible preaching. It is incipient, it seems to me, at an intellectually articulate level in the highly rationalistic condemnation of the rational in some neo-Orthodox circles. Whether here or in popular fundamentalism it is a reaction against liberalism, against the erasure of eschatology from the Gospel, against the almost enthusiastic experiment to discover how much amputation Christianity can survive under the surgical knife of modernity, against the religion of the social Gospel which turned out to be a secular ethic tinged with the sentiment of religion. These over a wide area were some of the effects of liberalism but not necessarily of the liberal temper at its best and as it has been represented by countless men noble in soul and enlightened in mind; for some sort of liberalism is the only antidote to the rigidity, the obscurantism, and the bigotry endemic to a dogmatic religion. Christianity is a dogmatic religion because it will not put Christ in the Pantheon and because it is a gospel of salvation by one Saviour alone. To suppose that there can be no liberal theology which does not betray this is to commit an arrogant injustice; and a romanticist one would be indeed to maintain that there have never been in Christian history, or that there never will be again, in the visible body of the Church, hardening of the mind against inconvenient truth and of the heart against reform. Again and again when official religion would not endure the peaceful solicitations of truth it has been shattered by the booming thunders of prophecy.

But sometimes, as in the reaction against liberalism, it seems that the thunders are not altogether divine. I think this is the case with what is often considered to be the pure Bible preaching. When it is eschatological at the level of American revivalism, it makes the Bible a timetable: it can tell you how to ascertain the end of the world, though our Lord distinctly said He didn't know. Where it is dogmatic and not governed by the liturgical year and the ethos of Catholic tradition, you will find, I think, rather generally, that it is so completely preoccupied with the Cross that the equally fundamental doctrines of the Incarnation and the Trinity receive scant treatment: the Christian Creed is virtually reduced to a single article. The great range of moral and ascetical theology is foreshortened in perspective to the experience of conversion and to petitionary prayer. It is, in a word, a Biblical preaching, so shut off from the main tradition of Christianity as to be unable to say, except on the most precariously subjective grounds, why these books and no other have the authority which is always, and very rightly, alleged for them.

Yet here we meet a curious paradox. There is no Bible preaching that is really undirected by some sort of tradition. There is always a point of view in interpretation and use which even in the most individualistic preachers is not exclusively their own. They represent groups or denominations, even the most modern of which have recognizable theologies. Only in the extreme periphery of humanistic liberalism and to the extent that the principle of authority is on principle repudiated will this appear not to be the case; yet even there a group tradition will have been formed or will be forming. I suppose in the end, considering the prior evil of our unhappy divisions, this is all to the good. There is no kind of Christian community for which the Bible is not somehow central and in which there is not some tradition that controls the estimate of the Bible's value and the use made of it.

Here, then, we come upon the present relevance of the *De Doctrina*. It conceives no preaching but Bible preaching. All doctrine, all moral theology, is rooted in Scripture and rises out of Scripture. But because he is sure that the public and continuous tradition of the Church concerning the Christian Faith is authentically derived from its Apostolic origin, Augustine, like other Fathers, assumes in all Scriptural interpretation an over-arching reverence for the teaching authority of the Church. There is in this an accurate perception of what is meant by the word *Canon,* an accurate perception of the process of determining the Canon, a process in which he was himself a participant. The definitive principle at work in the process is the principle of identifying those sacred books to which the Church owes obedience. So far as the New Testament is concerned, these books are by definition the originating documents of the Christian religion, and no other. By them the Church is bound to its origin not merely as beginning but as determinant. The Canon is an anchor chain, not an umbilical cord. At the same time, when you say "Canon," you are saying a great deal about the authority of the Church. You are saying, as the fact obliges you to say, that the Church has selected the contents of the Canon, that the Church has defined the authority of the Canon, and that the Church, by doing these things, has exercised "authority in controversies of faith." The Church is related to the Canon not only as a custodian or exhibitor, for this it could be with no responsibility beyond that of preserving a treasure of ancient documents. "It's all in the Book," yes, but in what Book? And how is it possible to contemplate this making of a Canon without discerning in it a high degree of dogmatic definition? Why were the contents of the New Testament limited to the writings of Apostles or their companions? It was because there was presumed to be a divine authority in the Apostolic witness and a testimony to the veracity of the Church's teaching contained in those writings which were by the consentient acknowledgment of the Churches received as Apostolic. Behind this there is moreover a conception of the Church's teaching and pastoral office as being derived from that of the Apostles. In this very confession of derivation, therefore, the Church sets up a bar of judgment before which it must stand in every age; and yet, when a man takes the Bible in his hand to criticize the Church, as the reformer must, in every age, he is holding in his hand the most all-embracing dogmatic definition that the Church has ever made.

All that I have endeavored to say has been directed to one end: to show that Christian preaching must be Bible-centered. This means that Holy Scripture is not used superficially, or casually, or merely for securing a kind of prestige of corroboration. Biblical preaching can be disfigured by an indiscriminate profusion of citation, but it cannot be at all without some citation or allusion or pervading echo of Holy Scripture. I think there would be little use in rules for the composition of Biblical sermons because the product of such rules would very likely be artificial or scholastic and extraordinarily dull. As a sermon, the Biblical sermon does not differ from any other kind, except in its impact on people in the lethargy of starvation for the authentic Word of God. The difference is not in the sermon but in the preacher. No man can preach or write but in the orientation of his own deepest presuppositions and preoccupation. If a priest stood at the altar arrayed in fine vestments and pink socks and brown shoes—need I press my parable? If a sermon is careless or dull or frigid or turbid with nothing to say but the commonplace, what is most conspicuous is that the pulpit is as empty as it was before the preacher went into it. But if the sermon does have something to say which is well said by an earnest man, what is most clearly heard is not so much what he says as what directs and controls what he has to say; and if any hearer, in the perplexity or conflict or yearning of his own human situation, hears what seems to him to become relevant to himself it is because, behind the preacher and underneath what the preacher says and above the immediacy of his own human need, he has discerned something that can transform him and give to his life a new direction and dimension. Whatever may be the controlling beliefs of a powerful orator, when he speaks the truth as he sees it, he has this effect on people: he moves them to be moved by what moves him.

Everything depends therefore on what I have called the orientation of the preacher, and of course he who would say what is right preaching must remember that his own orientation determines his judgment. I have presumed to offer to you my own presuppositions and I cannot then hide the conclusion to which they point. I do not see how it is possible to miss the significance of St. Augustine's concentration of attention upon Holy Scripture in telling the preacher what to preach and I do not see how it is possible to suppose that in doing this he considers the preacher to be independent of a great tradition of faith and practice. Here is not only Augustine but the common voice of the patristic Church. Positively it means that the preacher will be persuaded that the Holy Scriptures contain all Doctrine necessary for eternal salvation; that the preacher will himself be obedient to the Doctrine, the Sacraments, and the Discipline of Christ as the Church has received them, and that he will endeavor, in the elucidation of these as in his dealing with all human predicaments, to instruct the people out of the said Scriptures.

You recognize here our Ordinal for priests. I want you to, and I especially direct your meditation upon the word *out*. It is *out of* the Scriptures that you preach. You yourself must be immersed in them. No casual familiarity, no reading now and then, will do. If you seek to understand the soul of Scripture with your heart you will not be unduly anxious about the possible results of the undoubtedly extensive revolution [6] that has been going on in thought through a century of Biblical criticism and natural science and in human society in

[6] A useful discussion of some aspects of this "extensive revolution" will be found in *The Retreat from Christianity*, by the Rev. J. V. Langmead Casserley. Longmans, 1953.

what Toynbee calls "a time of troubles." You will not flee to some wretched hole of obscurantism and neither will you throw your Bible out of the window or put it on your shelf of the world's great literature. With the Church's faith in your heart, you cannot make of Bible preaching the playing of variations on a single tune, as though its eschatology were a timetable, or the states of the soul limited to a crisis of conversion. Your language will be noble because through it will sound the majestic rolling of the divine eloquence. Never, never will you seek to evade the demands of preaching next Sunday or wonder what you are to preach —not if the Scripture, the Creed, and the liturgical life of the Church are all livingly interwoven in your heart. You will be, though bound, exultant in your emancipation, for you will feel in you more to preach than you can ever say.

Ah, don't you want to preach? To describe to men the countenance of God? Prove to them that there is a God if you can. I do not say it is unimportant or unnecessary. But there is something better, for what you can show, you do not need to prove. This is something the great preachers knew, and the artists. First, of course, you will have to see it yourself. When a man sees Christ it does to him something terrible and wonderful, but until he has seen Christ in the Gospels, no matter how else he may see Him, he will not know who it is that he sees. And when he sees Christ he must also see the Law, for otherwise he will not understand why Christ died for him. And when he sees Christ he must also see the Prophets and the Apostles, for otherwise he will not know what dreadful and beautiful things God does with a man when He takes him in His hand, or what the Christian brotherhood must be and do. People will know whether we have seen by what we are. First look and then preach, for a man in some wise becomes what he sees if he loves what he sees. To preach, says Augustine, a man must understand the soul of Scripture with his heart, and what is the soul of Scripture but the revelation of the Face of Christ? Describing a mosaic head of our Lord in the cathedral of Cefalu, Ellery Sedgwick has written:

> There is the just and perfect judge. In all the great heads of Christ in mosaic the contours of the face are very similar; but this supreme figure

lacks the almost cruel inflexibility of other examples. In its place there is the serenity of consummate understanding, and of the impossibility of error, combined with the beauty of perfect sympathy. To every man sensible of sin such a countenance brings comfort and hope. There is not another expression like it in the whole world.[7]

Whence comes the recognition of the Saviour but from memory? Into the memory has flowed the experience of two millennia, all our own prayers and Communions, all we have known of holiness. It is the memory of the Church which becomes our memory, to which we refer all our own experience for its validity. And whence comes the memory of the Church but from the New Testament as it enshrines the testimony of the men who wrote it and who declared that by the word of the Lord Himself and by the illumination of the Holy Ghost they had perceived in the Old Testament a sure witness to Him and to the meaning of His Resurrection? Here is the anchor that holds the Church to the supreme moment within history, for we live, not by a dead remembrance, but by an ever-active

[7] "Sicilian Idyl," by Ellery Sedgwick. *Atlantic Monthly*, July, 1953.

recognition. Unless we preach from the Scriptures and revive amongst our people a familiarity with them, we uproot this essential recognition from the ground in which it grew and the only ground in which it can grow.

Lecture 2

THE USE OF IMAGES

THE AUTHOR of the *De Doctrina* is the author of the *De Civitate;* he who wrote of Christian rhetoric is he who wrote of the imperishable City of God while he saw before his eyes the dissolution of man's city. As a man, and a man of his time, and a Roman, he was no detached spectator of the latter; and as a Christian he could neither shut his heart nor close his eyes to that tidal wave of disaster which had already humbled the Imperial City, even then more than any other See the center of Western Christianity; which was engulfing churches in desolation and their people in death and famine; and which within a few short years was to begin with the violence of its inundation the erasure of Christian civilization from his own North Africa. The book he wrote was an apologia for Christianity in a time of troubles. Written in an age of apocalyptic upheaval and in the succession of Old Testament prophecy and the Revelation of St. John, it was, as Marcus Dods says, "the first real effort to produce a philosophy of history, to exhibit historical events in connection with their true causes, and in their real sequence." [1] Augustine states his purpose in these words:

> Rome having been stormed and sacked by the Goths under Alaric their king, the worshippers of false gods, or pagans as we commonly call them, made an attempt to attribute this calamity to the Christian religion, and began to blaspheme the true God with even more than their wonted bitterness and acerbity. It was this which kindled my zeal for the house of God, and prompted me to undertake the defense of the city of God against the charges and misrepresentations of its assailants. [2]

The true shape of disaster could only be discerned by a prophetic insight of the highest order; and only in the retrospect of history, after the world has recovered from it, can its effects upon

[1] From the Preface of his translation of *The City of God*, Post Nicene Fathers. The first part of the sentence is a quotation from Ozanam's *History of Civilization in the Fifth Century*.

[2] Philip Schaff, Editor, *Nicene and Post-Nicene Fathers*, Charles Scribner's Sons.

civilization and upon Christianity be estimated. At the time no man could watch it without deep disturbance: some were aghast, some tried to be optimistic, while fear spread in the populace. Let us listen to one man. I choose him because, as Joseph Cullen Ayer has said,

> Jerome's letters are not to be considered a primary source for the barbarian invasion, but they are an admirable source for the way the invasion appeared to a man of culture and some patriotic feeling.[3]

To this I may add that Jerome's consternation is the more striking in one who had withdrawn from the world, shaking from his shoes the dust of that Rome which he had considered so inhospitable to himself. In 396 he had anticipated the fall of Rome. In 409 he laments its imminence and the desolation of churches laid waste by the advancing storm. In the Preface of his Commentary on Ezekiel he contemplates the wreckage of its striking. I think you should hear these passages if you do not already

[3] Joseph Cullen Ayer, *A Source Book for Ancient Church History*, Charles Scribner's Sons, 1913. p. 422.

know them, and feel again their tragic impression if you do. Just before the fall of Rome he wrote:

> Innumerable savage tribes have overrun all parts of Gaul. The whole country between the Alps and the Pyrenees, between the Rhine and the ocean, has been laid waste. . . . The once noble city of Mainz has been captured and destroyed. In its church many thousands have been massacred. The people of Worms have been extirpated after a long siege. The powerful city of Rheims . . . Tournay, Speyer, and Strassburg have fallen to Germany. The Provinces of Aquitaine and of the Nine Nations, of Lyons and Narboone, with the exception of a few cities, all have been laid waste. Those whom the sword spares without, famine ravages within. I cannot speak of Toulouse without tears; it has been kept hitherto from falling by the merits of its revered bishop, Exuperius. Even the Spains are about to perish and tremble daily as they recall the invasion of the Cymri; and what others have suffered once, they suffer continually in fear.[4]

Then, after the Capital had fallen, he says:

> Who would believe that Rome, built by the conquest of the whole world, had collapsed; that

[4] Ayer, *op. cit.*

she had become both the mother of nations and their tomb;

But when the bright light of the whole world was put out, or rather when the Roman Empire was decapitated, and to speak more correctly, the whole world perished in one city, "I became dumb and humbled myself, and kept silence from good words, but my grief broke out afresh, my heart was hot within me, and while I was musing the fire was kindled." [5]

Now I should like you to consider a co-ordination of dates which I hope you will not think artificial because it seems to me highly significant for the purpose of this lecture. In 396 Jerome had anticipated catastrophe because it took no crystal ball to see it coming. In 397 Augustine began *The Christian Instruction* and shortly left it unfinished. In 410 Rome fell. From 413 to 426 Augustine was at work on *The City of God*. In 426 he completed *The Christian Instruction* with the treatise on rhetoric.

In what I have laid before you in the foregoing introduction to this lecture I believe I see an analogy, a parable in history. Permit me now to ex-

[5] Ayer, *op. cit.*

pound my parable beginning with the question, Why bother about rhetoric in an apocalyptic age? If any man asks why Christian preaching has any need of rhetoric at all, I will leave him to St. Augustine. Yet I shall have something later to say about this myself, though for the moment I cannot refrain from offering to my skeptical friend an admonitory quotation from *The Christian Instruction:*

> Now, the art of rhetoric being available for the enforcing either of truth or falsehood, who will dare to say that truth in the person of its defenders is to take its stand unarmed against falsehood? For example, that those who are trying to persuade men of what is false are to know how to introduce their subject so as to put the hearer into a friendly, or attentive, or teachable frame of mind, while the defenders of the truth are to be ignorant of that art? That the former are to tell their falsehoods briefly, clearly, and plausibly, while the latter shall tell the truth in such a way that it is tedious to listen to, hard to understand, and, in fine, not easy to believe in? That the former are to oppose the truth and defend falsehood with sophistical arguments, while the latter shall be unable either to defend what is true or to refute what is false? That the former, while im-

buing the minds of their hearers with erroneous opinions, are by their power of speech to awe, to melt, to enliven, and to rouse them, while the latter shall in defense of the truth be sluggish and frigid and somnolent? [6]

Now if anyone thinks that in the contemporary Christian scene the ascent of the preacher to the pulpit is generally a moment of electrifying expectation, let Augustine be to him, in the passage just quoted, as a heathen man and a publican. But if anyone believes that there has been in this country a decline in the quality and prestige of the pulpit and feels regret that the clergy are more highly esteemed as "leaders in the community" than as thinkers and prophets, he will find in this quotation something to reflect upon. To preach well requires far more than technique in the use of the voice, for if a man has nothing to say, it makes no difference how well he says it. And if he has no literary conscience, all the devices of psychology will make of him only a wheedler, a shouter, a sly user of popular clichés, a cunning practitioner on human minds and hearts even when he thinks he

[6] Schaff, *op. cit.*

is preaching the Gospel, because if the means are bad the end is poisoned.

However, the question that lies in my parable is not, Why bother with rhetoric? but rather, Why bother with it now? To say "now" signifies something urgent about our time, pressing, climactic. The words "we live in an apocalyptic time" have come to have a familiar sound. When whole cities can be dissolved in a single flash, when, to quote the late Senator Vandenburg, "the next war will be one that even the victors cannot afford to win," *now* becomes apocalyptic and the images of John's Revelation may well seem less monstrous than the features of fact. Everywhere there is the sense of imminence. We are like men waiting on the coast for a hurricane to strike. Hurricanes have struck before, and been survived, but this is one of unprecedented ferocity and scope. Hurricanes have also veered away to sea. So perhaps may this one. But man cannot control a hurricane, at least not yet. What is more terrible still is that he cannot control the hurricanes he makes in himself, in his own passions and in his own society. He engenders forces that leap out of his hands and go roaring over him with a rising momentum that gives to them at least the plausible appearance of historical inevitability. In this *now* the storm warnings are everywhere unmistakable and the barometer is low. We have no time for eloquence as a luxury item.

But what I am eager for you to see and ponder is that in another time of storm and stress the greatest Christian of his age did not at all consider eloquence to be a luxury item, or the study of it a trivial pursuit. Surely there is something significant, not only for him but for us, in his resuming *The Christian Instruction* in the same year in which he completed *The City of God*. He thought it urgently necessary for the Gospel to be preached with clear, artistic, and moving eloquence. Is it less urgent now? When you are instituted into your parish can you pray with your tongue in your cheek for "a readiness of thought and expression suitable to the clearness and excellency" of God's Holy Word? Excellency is a sonorous word; it raises great thoughts, of grandeur and majesty and sovereignty. These are the attributes of God, and in the fourth chapter of The Revelation of St.

John, the God of Majesty is worshipped. In the fifth, it is the same God who is adored but the majesty is seen in the new light of sacrificial love, for there is in the midst of the Throne a Lamb as it had been slain: "And they sung a new song, saying, Thou art worthy to take the book, and to open the seals thereof: for thou wast slain, and hast redeemed us to God by thy blood out of every kindred, and tongue, and people, and nation; And hast made us unto our God kings and priests: and we shall reign on the earth" (Rev. 5:9-10). How shall a man speak suitably to this? What is a readiness of thought suitable to this? Not only here, yet sublimely here, is the Gospel. If one says, "The preaching of the Gospel requires eloquence," one can be saying something abstract, as though one were to exhibit bones and say, "Here is a man." But the Gospel is scarcely at all a definition or a formula. It is a picture. Revelation requires seeing. The Incarnation is the picture of God, yet not so to speak in still-life; it is the picture of God doing and of His being immanent in and perceptible through His doing. Will you think me fanciful if I say that preaching is the showing of a motion picture with commentary that helps to understand but does not intrude, and that sometimes the picture is to be shown moving and sometimes, perhaps of necessity more often, as a filmstrip? Each Sunday, and especially on the great Feasts, you stop the movement of the film and show one picture alone; yet always, as your people gaze on each individual scene, you must help them to remember and to feel the movement, the meaning, of the whole story. This you cannot do without imagination.

Imagination is seeing a picture with the inward eye. It has been defined as "the illusion of the higher reality" and in this, illusion does not mean hallucination. "Heaven," said Jaubert, "seeing that there are many things which by our nature we cannot know, has given us the faculty of imagining them." This is by no means anti-intellectual. It allows to the discursive intellect its province as it moves by rational process from what is known to what may therefrom be inferred; and if there is to be allowed any validity to human knowledge, there must be allowed also the possibility of authentic observation. Here to be sure is the field of epistemology, but in that field care should be taken not to explain away the epistemologist. How skeptical can you be? The Church has a huge stake in the defense of the human intellect, for it holds that man must worship God with his mind, and in the face of a lot of prevalent self-decapitating skepticism, it can afford to press its case with a sense of humor as well as with learning. Yet at the last the Church is talking about a transcendent reality which the intellect can grasp only, as it must grasp anything, by abstraction. This gives its domain to theology, for the Church must talk about God, and theology must do so in its own way, as Victor Hugo said of music, since it must say that which a man cannot utter yet concerning which he cannot keep silent. But the experience itself, about which theology discourses, does not come by way of the discursive intellect. It comes by a way of its own, as what is now so often spoken of as confrontation: he looks at me and I look at him. You remember, those are the words of a peasant. One does not need to be a peasant, but neither does one need to be an intellectual.

Does one need faith? Afterwards, yes, but not before, for faith is response. Shall I not say that the revelation of God offers to me the opportunity for faith, the capacity for faith even here where I stand in whatever blindness of sin; in the very revealing God plants in me a seed of faith, which by grace I may nourish or by obstinate refusal I may kill. Once aroused and being kept alive faith becomes in me the capacity to recognize and obey God wherever subsequently I meet Him.

So many and such great men have debated the nature of faith as to give one the impression that it cannot be comprehended in a single definition. Is it then so complex? In the effort to analyze it, it seems so, or rather it seems to be elusive of analysis. Is it intellectual assent, is it supra-rational insight, is it a supernatural gift, or is it in the original nature of man the adventurous starting point of all knowledge and all action, or is it again trust and self-commitment? Can it not be that there are many modes of its operation, especially since in the New Testament it is used in more than one connotation? Can it not be—how shall I say it, that faith is a composer of the soul's activity rather than a component in it?—not something in addition to other faculties and operations, but something that directs all of them and as it were gathers them together? It is easier to define a drop of water than to define the sea. In every language men have words for the ultimates of their experience and of these it is least possible to say what they are, not because they are the last things men come to, but because they are the first; they are everywhere present, they pervade everything. Perhaps the most familiar are triads: truth, beauty, and goodness; faith, hope, and charity. They are triads because they are not separate, yet distinct. It is easier to recognize them than to define them.

Now I wanted to bring you to St. Paul's triad. They are the gifts of the Spirit; they are the greatest gifts, transcending all others. Yet they operate in man's nature which was created by God, was dead to sin, and has been raised in Christ. There is a new man but not another man. They operate together because they abide together. You cannot love what you wholly do not know, or hope for it, or have faith in it—or Him. And knowing must in some wise have seeing. In some wise. There is a kind of sight that faith does not need and indeed in this life cannot have. There is a blessing on those who have not seen and yet have believed. No man hath at any time seen God save in the revelation of His only-begotten Son. And the first Disciples saw with their eyes what we cannot. But is there then no sight for us? The Epistle to the Hebrews tells us that there is a "solid certainty" of things unseen, and bids us look unto Jesus. St. Paul tells us that there is a seeing here, though dimly as in a mirror, but then in unclouded vision. In the Beatific Vision we shall see what we have seen and yet what we have not seen. There is in some wise seeing because there has been a revelation.

But the seeing is by means of a mirror *en ainigmati*. The old translation was "darkly," the new is "dimly," and there seems to be some overtone of meaning that a single word cannot embrace. The ordinary translation of *ainigma* is "riddle," but that does not easily go with mirror. But at all events what do you have in a mirror? Is it not an illusion, but an authentic illusion of the reality there reflected? At the present time, says the Apostle, that is all there is, there isn't any more until *then;* but what is now seen—for even the natural mind can discern the everlasting power and divinity of God through the things that are seen—is an image of reality. At no point in his earthly life does man experience the spiritual as purely spiritual and at no point is his subjective impression of it without image. By a process of reflection and inquiry he explores the meaning of the image and endeavors by the criticism of his impressions of reality to estimate their validity. This is the field of science and of theology. If it were not for this exploration and criticism, there would arise no enigma in the image, for he would suppose that what he thinks he sees is exactly what is. There is indeed no escape from the enigma nor yet from the image. If man does not criticize his image, that is to say, if he does not recognize that it is an image, he will worship it and as easily change the substance of the eternal God into the figments of his mind as into the works of his hands. Yet, on the other hand, if he thinks to find the truth by the abandonment of the image and to perceive it purely in the intellectual concept, he comes to a desert where all is empty sky and barren sand.

God has been good to us. Seeing that by our nature we cannot know what is not revealed, he bids us seek what may be found and meets our seeking with a showing. Because no man hath seen God nor can, and yet because man cannot rest until he sees God, he has not been left to the inventions of fancy or to the hypotheses of reason; for the Word was made flesh and dwelt among us, and we have beheld His glory. The Christian Creed is not a set of propositions, but a story. The Incarnation is a picture of God, yet our Lord came not simply for a showing but to do a deed so that, as Juliana of Norwich so lovingly said, "all thing shall be well and all manner of thing shall be well." The center of Christian worship is an action; that it is choreographic in the greatest solemnities of its performance is in a way true, but it differs from any merely dramatic action because what is being recalled is present, He who is forever Priest and Lamb is there as Priest and Lamb, and the action which it represents is there operative. All of this is image. Since man can only know reality in image, and since he dare not make his own or worship it, God has given him the image under the seal of the Resurrection of our Blessed Redeemer and by the authentication of the Holy Spirit of truth.

I propose to you that there is a profound misapprehension of the Old Testament in supposing it to be directed to the abolition of image. It does indeed condemn idolatry and forbids also the making of the image or likeness not only of God but of anything at all. There is about this something so absolute and yet at the same time so paradoxical in its application that it must not be explained simply in its historical relevance. I mean to say that it is not enough to point out that the prohibition is aimed wholly at preceding levels of religion or at the dangers of contamination from surrounding cults. By any kind of idolatry the revelation of God is shackled to the representation; it is unable to move beyond the apprehension there achieved unless it destroys the image. Even primitive people do not so much think that the idol is God as that God inhabits it. Inevitably God is shrunk to the form of the image. But there is something else, and it is far worse. In everything that man makes there is an imitation of reality and a kind of capture of reality. In all that he makes man seems to himself to achieve a power, a mastery that swallows up reverence in an absurd confidence in his own manipulations whether by ritual or by technics. Do you have to go to the ancient Near East to study idolatry? After a century of its most outrageous absurdity, when the universe needed no God so long as man was there with his machinery, we are perhaps no longer sure that we are God, and indeed, we are not altogether sure that we are human.

But man has to make. He has to make in his mind as well as with his hands. It is quite impossible for him not to make the likeness of something on the earth and with the imaging of his mind and the imitation of his art not to make a likeness of what is in Heaven above. But it is all under judgment, because it is from his imagination and his making that his delusions work and it is in them too that he sins with his will. Therefore must they be condemned, and therefore must they be redeemed.

It is quite easy to understand the second Commandment in relation to ancient idolatries. It is even easy to understand the Iconoclastic controversy in the Church. But when you look at the matter in a universal perspective, you will see, I think, that St. John of Damascus was more right than we had perhaps perceived. Images are inevitable because man is what he is; they are under judgment because he has sinned; they are indispensable because he is man. The Temple had no effigy of God, but it had a liturgy and a ceremonial, and nowhere is there a literature more picturesque than the Old Testament. It is ridiculous to say that images and likenesses are made only with the hands in sculpture or painting. Images are in architecture, in ritual, in music, in the dance, in history, in poetry, in biography—in everything, because they arise in the mind. They arise in the mind as pictures, still or moving, of all that creates experience and they are, moreover, the basic, all-determinative symbols, no less than the vehicles, of apprehended meaning. Discursive examination of them is separate from them. The experience itself never is. They are the illusion of reality, the way it impinges on the human mind. Religion without them is impossible, a religious literature without them—and I am not speaking of theological literature, which is quite another thing—scarcely could exist; and preaching without them is dead on its feet.

Now eloquence stirs the imagination. It brings to the hearer the reality of which it speaks. It does this when it teaches no less than when it delights, for it delights while it teaches. A dull discourse may be quite precise theologically and clear in its use of language but since it does not appear to have enlivened the speaker it positively discourages interest in the hearer. There is a very great need for the accurate teaching of doctrine, and this is done, as Augustine says, in the subdued manner, with reasonableness and clarity; yet what saves it from the irrelevance of abstraction is the punctuating flash of insight by which this manipulation of concepts comes alive as the concern of living men. Are you expounding Eucharistic doctrine? Then listen to John Donne: "Who can fear death this night, that hath had the Lord of Life in his hand today?" Are you preaching on the Incarnation? Then you must let me see how that this is no masquerade, no play-acting, of God, and no graduating into divinity of a holy man. How is Jesus different from the rest of us, and how is He like the rest of us? I do not think this can be done without some imagination, "For God, who commanded the light to shine out of darkness, hath shined in our hearts, to give the light of the knowledge of the glory of God in the face of Jesus Christ."

As an art, eloquence is a work of the imagination.

It requires a deep respect for words and for form and structure in the combination of words. It recognizes that ideas have polarity, mutual coherence, and mutual repugnance; yet it can never touch ideas without somehow incarnating them, without transforming even the insubstantial concept into something as it were sensory. Of all the media of imagery, language is at once the richest and the most articulate. It is the one form of ecclesiastical art that the poorest congregation need not do without. The use of art, sincerely and seriously, is from the earliest times inseparable from the expression of Christianity: in places of worship for the remembrance of the Sacred Story, and in the ministry of the Word for the proclamation of the Sacred Story. If churches are needed in this or any age, eloquence is needed also.

Eloquence, in Christian use and purpose, must have characteristics proper to itself. Speaking of these characteristics, Archbishop Brilioth says:

> It is perhaps not too bold to say that it is a feature peculiar to the biblical religion to give to the spoken word a place in the worship of the religious community, as one of its essential elements, and that this gives to the Christian sermon a

unique character. It has grown to be a specific type of rhetoric, distinct from other forms of speaking, or perhaps eloquence. And I would suggest, as a working hypothesis which has to be tested by an historical study, that the distinctive character of the sermon consists in these three elements which we have found in our Lord's sermon in the synagogue of Nazareth:

(1) the liturgical—it forms a part of divine service and is itself a mode of worship;

(2) the expository, or exegetical—it starts from and expounds a text from Scripture;

(3) the prophetic—it is a message for the present time, making the Scripture text a living word in the actual situation.[7]

While at any occasion of Christian worship there may be a sermon, perhaps conceived as something added, in the liturgy the sermon has been from the earliest times an integral element. The first reference to this is in Acts 20:7. In his second-century account of the Eucharist, Justin specifically includes the sermon in the structure of the rite between the lections and the common prayers. In our own Prayer Book "the" sermon is provided for at the Eucharist and nowhere else is there direction for

[7] *Landmarks in the History of Preaching*, by Ynge Brilioth. S.P.C.K., 1950.

a sermon except at Ordinations and at the Institution of Ministers, where, in both cases, there is a Eucharist.

Because of the sermon's place in the liturgy, its Scriptural grounding receives a heightened significance. Holy Scripture informs and conditions Christian worship no less than it determines Christian doctrine. The Bible reverberates through all the Church's offices, and dominates them. In the Eucharist, the Upper-Room narratives dictate its meaning and purpose, while deeply imbedded lies the profound typological meaning of the Exodus and of the Creation story. The Bible is not for Christians a merely "Jewish" literature, but the Sacred Books of the New and the True Israel.

If the sermon, then, does not speak with a Scriptural voice it violates the liturgy of which it presumes to be an element. By being itself alien from Scripture, in content, in utterance, and in its whole method of thinking, it gives to the people the impression that the Bible is alien to them as something merely ancient, hard to understand, and probably irrelevant, with the result that the liturgy also becomes to them a dead language.

To speak with the voice of Scripture is something else entirely from a mere drenching of the sermon in Scriptural allusion or quotation. Allusion and quotation there must be, if the Bible is again to live in the religion of the people, but always with discernment and the rigorous discipline of thought that is consonant with the reference. I need scarcely say that a spurious imitation of Biblical language is an impertinence that will only disgust the hearers: they may recognize the lion's skin but they will also recognize the voice of the ass. To preach in a manner suitable both to the Bible and the Church, the preacher must himself move freely and as being himself at home, in the whole way of thinking and expression that belongs to the Bible. This carries with it a use of Scripture not so much to prove the teaching of the Church as to show it: for if you would win acceptance of Christian doctrine you have to show the things *behind* the things of which you are directly speaking. To do this you must strike into the imagination of your hearers, and this is what Holy Scripture most consummately does.

It does so by the concreteness of its thought and

expression; that is to say, by the image rather than by an abstraction or a generalized idea. This does not mean at all that the "universal" or the "eternal" or "the principle" is absent; but it is certainly not present in the mode of Greek thinking. Always, the particular carries the meaning of the general, the instance that of the principle; and history, action, story with movement in time is the vehicle of the eschatological reality. Let me draw your attention to some examples.

Here is one, not carefully selected but chosen quite at random, from a thousand others that are like it. It is picturesque, not by the use of metaphor or figure, but by its straightforward description in the plainest kind of speech.

> He that walketh righteously, and speaketh uprightly; he that despiseth the gain of oppressions, that shaketh his hands from holding of bribes, that stoppeth his ears from hearing of blood, and shutteth his eyes from seeing evil; He shall dwell on high: his place of defence shall be the munitions of rocks: bread shall be given him; his waters shall be sure. Thine eyes shall see the king in his beauty: they shall behold the land that is very for off.—Isaiah 33:15–17

Now put beside this the narrative of our Lord's Temptation. It is brief, and is no "fancy" language. But you can *see* it. Unless it is spurious, it is one of His most intimate disclosures to His disciples. All that it may mean can fill a thousand books of moral theology which graciously He did not write. You cannot for a moment suppose that He invented the imagery as a "device of communication." He told them what had happened; but all that it had meant to Him and all that it could mean to them and to us lies in a mystery for meditation in the way He told it. Imagery, something seen, something happening, that takes hold of the imagination, does not necessarily depend on metaphor or figurative language. Indeed, too much of this will make discourse languid and misty and prove a very sedative to the imagination. The preacher must strive for description that really describes, for narrative that really tells a story, for language that is plain, vigorous, and vivid.

At the same time, there is a place for metaphor and for figurative language. The Bible has this also in profusion. But it does not cloy because it is always vivid. Our Lord's most remembered teaching is by story and by likeness. What is the Kingdom of God? He does not define it. But He says, it is like this, it is like that; listen to this story, now to this. In the Fourth Gospel, as there are the Seven Signs, so there are the Seven Symbols: I am the Vine, I am the Good Shepherd, and the rest. Yet for all this, what He says is neither obscure nor indirect, except to them who will not believe that He means what He says, or who, perceiving what he means, are outraged by it. When, over the Bread, He says, "This is my Body," whatever it means it certainly does *not* mean "this is *not* my Body." The more you reflect on the Gospels, the more, I think, you will be persuaded that the images of Christ's expression are the images of His own thought and that He does not intend to permit His thought to be so abstracted from them as to leave the images themselves to be discarded by His disciples. His words will not pass away because they enshrine His meaning in the way He wished it to be understood. Among those images which appear in His own thought are Lucifer falling as lightning, John Baptist as "Elijah that cometh if ye are able to receive it," the Covenant People, the Davidic Kingdom,

Zion the City of God, and the prophetic figures of the Son of Man and the Servant. He who would preach Christ for the world or for modern man, and who shuffles off these images as though they were merely the historical costume of the Incarnation, will be preaching precisely what he thinks he has saved himself from, that is, a mythological Christ, some kind of modern myth.

The unfolding revelation of the Bible is dominated by images of fact and event. I have already mentioned some of the most powerful of these as forming the thought of Jesus. I wish now to speak of the development of the image, the way the revelation grows towards its fulfillment by this development.

To do this we embark on the recital of a story the central Figure of which is the Man who is the Servant of God. The story begins at the Creation, with the existence of the heavens and the earth, and it concerns itself not with how they came to be, except that they came to be through God's Word, but with why they came to be. This *why* does not appear from nature. It appears out of the religious experience of Israel, and that is an experience of

Redemption and of Providence. The God who redeems and sustains is the Creator. In the midst of the waste and the vast He calls out order and movement and life which but for His sustaining power would collapse into chaos. Man emerges as the crown of creation, and made from the stuff of it, to bring it all, and himself in it, into the Rest of God in the ordered Liturgy of the Sabbath. The purpose of creation is the rejoicing of all things in the praise of God: "O all ye works of the Lord, Bless ye the Lord: praise Him and magnify Him forever."

But man fell from his true estate. Created to be the priest of nature, its intellect and articulate voice, he makes himself unfit for his ministry, making thereby the whole creation the victim of his fall. Yet for all this God does not abandon either him or His Creation. He holds out to him a covenant in Abraham and by Moses, a covenant of promise and of redemption; and this is for all men, and not only for the Jew; for in Abraham all the families of the earth shall be blessed. By the promise to Abraham, by the redemption wrought in the Exodus and the Passover by Moses, and by the Kingdom of David, God called Israel to be the Servant.

But they turned it all to their own sin and to their own pride until at last the Holy City was trodden under foot of the Gentiles and the Temple of God was destroyed. Then did Ezekiel see the Glory of God in the Cloud move from the threshold of the Temple, and above the doomed City, till it stood over the "mountain on the east of the City." So the Glory departed, yet to come again upon the New Temple, where when it entered in at the threshold "the Cloud filled the House." Israel shall again be gathered, and all nations shall come to worship the true and living God; and there is the radiance of one like a Son of Man who shall bring the people of the saints of the Most High to present them to the Ancient of Days.

> For as the new heavens and the new earth, which I will make, shall remain before me, saith the Lord, so shall your seed and your name remain. And it shall come to pass, that from one new moon to another, and from one sabbath to another, shall all flesh come to worship before me, saith the Lord.—Isaiah 66:22–23

With this Christianity begins. This is the story out of which it grew. Hear now the same story as it is told by the New Israel in the light of Christ.

In the beginning was the Word, and without Him there was nothing, for all things were made by Him. Though He was in the Form of God, He made Himself of no reputation and took upon Himself the Form of the Servant and was found in the likeness of men. He is the new Adam, the new Man. He is the seed of Abraham, the true son of Abraham to whom the promise was made. "He was faithful to him who appointed him, just as Moses also was faithful in God's house. . . . Moses was faithful in all God's house as a servant . . . but Christ was faithful over God's house as a son" (Heb. 3:2, 5–6, R.S.V.). To Him is given the Kingdom of His father David, a kingdom not of this earth though the things of this earth are to be brought into it. In Him, as the Messiah, Israel as the servant of God is concentrated in the one Man who is the Servant in the perfection of His obedience. He came to call Israel to be truly Israel; but as of old they heeded not the Prophets so now they heeded not the Prince. Yet the Covenant shall not fall to the ground. Now, by Him, it is made new in His own blood, by a true and living sacrifice of which the old sacrifice was a type and a shadow.

74

Now, by Him and in the New Covenant, will be fulfilled the expectation of the Prophets, "Rejoice, ye Gentiles, with His People": for the wall of partition is cast down and the Court of the Gentiles is cleansed for their coming to stand before God. The iniquity of Jerusalem is full to the brim, and in the Lord's weeping over her and in her murder of Him, her destruction is already present. Yet murderous Jerusalem is supremely hallowed by His death, for that City "which spiritually is called Sodom and Egypt, where also our Lord was crucified" *is* the Holy City, though the true Jerusalem is above and cometh down from God; and this is the City which is free, and is the mother of us all. From the City that was desolate the Apostles saw ascending to His throne the victorious King, the accepted Servant, the Man, enveloped in the Cloud of the Glory of the Lord. The Temple is already raised up from its destruction, for it is His Body, indwelt by the Holy Spirit, wherein are offered spiritual gifts and sacrifices, by men of every race and nation, "who have tasted the heavenly gift, and have become partakers of the Holy Spirit, and have tasted the goodness of the word of God and the powers of the age to come" (Heb. 6:4-5, R.S.V.). For this age to come *will* come again in the Cloud of the Glory to gather the people of the saints of the Most High before the Ancient of Days in the rest that remaineth for the people of God. And then shall the whole creation bless the Lord.

Christian preaching must be "relevant" to this. It must tell the Church's story and be attuned to the images with which the Sacred Scriptures clothe it. The Creed is a synopsis of the story, and the liturgical action is the recitation of its essential elements in prayer and thanksgiving. In liturgies of the Antiochene group it is more detailed, and in Western liturgies derived from Rome more abbreviated. But here is the oldest liturgy we know, that of Hippolytus:

> We give thee thanks, O God, through Thy beloved Son Jesus Christ, Whom in the last days Thou didst send to us, a Savior and Redeemer, and Angel of Thy counsel: Who is Thy inseparable Word, through Whom Thou didst make all things, and He was well pleasing unto Thee: Thou didst send Him from heaven into the womb of a Virgin: He was conceived and became incarnate, and was shown to be Thy Son,

being born of the Holy Spirit of a Virgin: Who, fulfilling Thy will and acquiring a holy people for Thee, stretched out His hands for suffering that He might free from suffering those who believed in Thee. And when He was betrayed to His voluntary passion, that He might loose the pains of death and break the chains of the devil, might tread underfoot the power of Hell and lead forth the righteous, fix the boundary thereof and make known His Resurrection, taking bread. . . . [And then follow the Words of Institution].

"Relevant" looks in two directions. If the Gospel is preached in such a way that its story and its images are treated, on the one hand with contemptuous disregard, or on the other as though they are merely to be preserved amid lavender and old lace, as though either they are capable of no living interpretation, or had no need of any interpretation, such a preaching has no authentic Christian message for living men. We shall have more to say in the next lecture about relevance to our time and our situation. People are of course conditioned by the culture in which they live and our culture has much the appearance of being "post Christian." Certainly the Bible is not as much an accepted authority as it was but a little while ago. Protestant Christianity is not deeply affected by the liturgical tradition, and the Liturgical Movement among Catholics shows that much is amiss and needs renewal. The current images of speech and thought make it often difficult for Christian images to penetrate the minds of those we preach to. But this constitutes the problem and the challenge for Christian eloquence. If you stand —as you must, unless you are a liar and a cheat— on the Bible, the Creed, and the Prayer Book, there can be no doubt what it is in which you must find the relevance.

In any event, if the culture of what was Christendom is, so far as it may be, inhospitable to the Christian story and the Christian images, how has it become so? How does it come, then, that vast multitudes in this country alone should seek the prophetic revelation of destiny and the realization of Christian brotherhood quite outside of what we sometimes call "the respectable churches"? How does it come that multitudes in countries anciently Christian should seek the satisfaction of essentially Christian aspirations in a life-philosophy that positively repudiates Christ? Where was the watchman, and

where was the messenger, and where was the steward! What have we been doing and what have we
been saying for a hundred years? The life and witness of the Church must have been at least defective
enough to merit some deserved reproach and to
afford pretext for much that is undeserved. Perfect
it cannot be in this world, but the Church could
have been and could be now better than it is. As
young men must always fight and die in wars they
did not make, so now you must go forth to recover
provinces that should not have been lost, to bleed
for wrongs you did not do, and, please God, to win
victories your fathers did not win. Can you go
without the sword of the Spirit, which is the
Word of God? Now Christ is *Verbum Dei,* the
Word from everlasting to everlasting, uttered in
the Creation of the universe, ineradicably written
in all that He has made, spoken to men whether
they will hear or whether they will forbear. In
Him, as we may say, the silence of eternity becomes
audible. You will perhaps think here of the striking
words of St. Ignatius of Antioch:

> And hidden from the prince of this world was
> the virginity of Mary and her child-bearing and

likewise also the death of the Lord—three mysteries to be cried aloud—the which were wrought in the silence of God.[8]

But Christ is also *Sermo Dei*, for by His Incarnation, and in all He said and did, He has expounded the Divine Word in the language of men. He enters into a colloquy with us, and cries to us, "Why will ye die?" His Incarnation is the divine eloquence in which God pleads with man and welcomes him, though a sinner. What human eloquence is worthy of this—yet, of what eloquence it is worthy!

[8] *To the Ephesians*, 19.

Lecture 3

PREACHING IN A TIME
OF ANXIETY

LET US BEGIN today with something already spoken of which I think nobody will dispute: we live in a time of global and simultaneous revolution in all human affairs. It is historically what Toynbee calls "a time of troubles." In some respects, though possibly not in all, this revolution is greater than any that has taken place in the last six thousand years. In human thought, wherever the full tide of it is felt—and the tide is gathering all men into it—the revolutionary forces of recent centuries as it were come together. The Copernican revolution moved the earth from the center of the universe and brought to man a diminished sense of his own cosmic centrality among created beings. This is now further diminished by the possibility, if not the likelihood, that organic beings, of an even higher development than his own, exist elsewhere in the universe or may hereafter in cosmic time exist in profusion after his little biography is closed. The physical continuity of man with the evolutionary history of organic life on this planet has been established, for man is a mammal and a vertebrate; and it may very well turn out, as research goes on, that there is psychological continuity as well, at any rate to an extent far greater than we have hitherto supposed. On every continent social revolution is simultaneous and interactive, and nowhere can its pains and its potentiality be more clearly seen than in Africa, the continent where only an hour ago, so to speak, man seemed to be unchangeably primitive. Masses of men are on the march for emancipation from ancient and long repressions, to assert the significance of their existence and to claim their place on earth. "Inferior" races, subject races, everywhere arise, and only the white man seems still unaware that the world is not white and will never again be white, unless by some Mendelian trick of racial fusion everybody becomes white. Yet, in a singular irony, the century and a half which can be called the epoch of emancipation, and which, in what *was*

Christendom, rejoiced increasingly in man's omni-competence, has conjured up the monstrous spectre of an infra-human State, everywhere possible, everywhere germinating, that denies to man any dignity whatever beyond that of the ant and the bee, and, in E. E. Cummings' satirical phrase, seeks "the salvation of all by the assassination of each."

Two world wars and the atomic bomb have shaken man's self-assurance. But this is not all gain. There has been growing a deep doubt of the human, an uncertainty as to "what it *were* to be a man," to use Aristotle's phrase. This is the measure of the repudiation of Christianity, and, I am afraid, to some extent, of the failure of Christianity in the modern world. Aristotle could scarcely have phrased his question otherwise than in the subjunctive because he had not seen Jesus; but for Christendom to doubt what it *is* to be a man could come only by forgetfulness or repudiation. I think perhaps that like the Gadarene inhabitants we have besought the Lord to depart from among us because we lost some pigs by His presence. The loss of intellectual control over western civilization could hardly have occurred if there had not preceded it a loss of moral control, a weakening of the central edifice of religion.

And this in turn cannot be blamed on the Reformation, which itself could not have taken place in a society deeply devoted to the Church as the Reformation found it. In the countries which the Reformation did not win, the movement of counter-revolution was itself the recognition of decadence. If we are to look for the causes of estrangement between contemporary western culture and Christianity, we should look to the eighteenth century. There, among the curious cross-currents of that complex century, we must fix our attention on at least two things that were freighted with trouble. The first was the indifference of established Christianity to the revolutionary aspirations of the common people. The second was the emergence and rapid development of naturalism in many forms. Naturalism grew fat subsequently on the food of corroboration supposedly provided by all the natural sciences, and the more so because from the time of Galileo established Christianity had abdicated any right of interpretation. It should be said to the credit of liberalism that it saw the tragedy of abdication. These men knew that it was as much cowardice and folly to try to hide from a discrepancy in the Bible or a fossil in the ground as from the movements of the planets. Their interpretations and their conclusions are inadequate and, if you please, often erroneous; but their gesture was noble. Never more than now must their gesture be imitated. I want to read to you an interpretation of the "facts of life," which include of course the facts of science. It has been often quoted. It is a singularly lofty piece of prose writing, by Bertrand Russell.

> That Man is the product of causes which had no prevision of the end they were achieving; that his origin, his growth, his hopes and fears, his loves and his beliefs, are but the outcome of accidental collocations of atoms; that no fire, no heroism, no intensity of thought and feeling, can preserve an individual life beyond the grave; that all the labors of the ages, all the devotion, all the inspiration, all the noonday brightness of human genius, are destined to extinction in the vast death of the solar system, and that the whole temple of Man's achievement must inevitably be buried beneath the debris of a universe in ruins—

all these things, if not quite beyond dispute, are yet so nearly certain, that no philosophy which rejects them can hope to stand. Only within the scaffolding of these truths, only on the firm foundation of unyielding despair, can the soul's habitation henceforth be safely built.[1]

If this interpretation of the facts is indeed "if not quite beyond dispute, yet so nearly certain" that no philosophy of life can reject it and stand, despair is undoubtedly the only outcome. The despair can take many forms in action. It can be vicious, criminal, and mad. It can be inert, resigned, or gross in laying hold of the present moment. It can be tragic and exalted, and being deprived of God and of eternity, it can produce the only elevation of character which is then possible; for, as the same writer says further:

In this lies Man's true freedom: in determination to worship only the God created by our own love of the good, to respect only the heaven which inspires the insight of our best moments.[2]

[1] Bertrand Russell, *Mysticism and Logic*. Copyright 1929 by W. W. Norton & Company.

[2] Cf: "Man has his highest being, his God, in himself; not in himself as an individual, but in his essential nature, his species. No individual is an adequate representative of his species, but only the human individual is conscious of the distinction between the

Do not despise this: for it sets forth something of the utmost seriousness to which your preaching must be directed; and also it sets forth something both more honorable and more heroic than the life-attitude that lurks beneath much superficial Christianity.

In the face of what surrounds us, the task of preaching and of the pastoral ministry is what it has always been yet with a special and contemporary relevance. This task is to create anxiety where there is none, to move it from chimeras to reality and from the things that matter least to those that matter most, and to proclaim the place of assurance that both uses and absorbs anxiety. In such a setting, the spiritual works of mercy can be performed only with deep searchings of the preacher's own heart, with an integrity that spurns all tricks and pious deceptions, and with love. To instruct the ignorant, to counsel the doubtful, to comfort the mourners remain but a fragmentary assistance

species and the individual; in the sense of this distinction lies the root of religion. The yearning of man after something above himself is nothing else than the longing after the perfect type of his nature, the yearning to be free from himself, i.e., from the limits and defects of his individuality." Ludwig Feuerbach, *The Essence of Christianity*.

until a soul has been truly centered upon God who Himself alone can give "beauty for ashes, the oil of gladness for mourning, and the garment of praise for the spirit of heaviness." To fix your heart on this will carry you into studies wide and deep and into the lofty solitudes of prayer which, however, are not solitude, for there you choose your company and discover yourself most graciously chosen to be a companion. There will be no time for inanities and for those pleasant little ten-minute talks to congregations looking at their watches, for if you truly preach the Word of God you will learn, perhaps with grateful surprise, that your people have forgotten that they own watches; and if you prepare your sermons to say what then and there can be said, you will not impose upon their patience. In this connection, remember that, as Prodicus said laughing, a speech must be neither long nor short, but of a convenient length.

But that is relatively unimportant. What is important is integrity; and if you wonder why I so often use that word, it is because without it eloquence is a great tool of the devil. Plato's estimate of rhetoric is lower than Augustine's, but they agree that the first rule of speaking is truthfulness. Rhetoric, says Socrates, is only an art of persuasion, though other arts also persuade, and it produces belief, not knowledge. This is not to say that it cannot produce knowledge, if what is said is true; but of itself as an art eloquence aims only at persuasion to accept what is said. The disingenuous man, then, who is an orator, can do more mischief than a clumsy speaker. Yet integrity is not infallibility, and for that reason it requires of the preacher, particularly if he has a Catholic conscience, a moral endeavor of the most exacting kind. If you speak for the Church, you must speak what the Church speaks. Well, then, your troubles are over, for, provided you are sure that St. Thomas is always right, you have only to read his works to your people in twenty-minute bites and you will be guilty of no heresy. If, on the contrary, you have only to take up the Bible with no responsibility to the Church in liturgy or dogma, you can with a clear conscience prophesy from Sunday to Sunday —though why on Sunday rather than Saturday would be an interesting question—out of your own inspired interpretation.

But if you wish to be faithful to the Church whose minister you are and at the same time to be a man and not a phonograph record, you must encounter the difference between the responsibility of an ambassador and the responsibility of a slave. What you preach can be alive, contemporary, and a genuine communication of the Divine Word when it is *yours*. Why else should Augustine write his book around the interpretation of Scripture? The very nature of interpretation is that it takes risks, that it says something which is not identical with what it interprets. The problem, then, of integrity—if indeed it is a problem at all— is the problem of the calculated risk. The preacher himself in his ordination to the priesthood is a calculated risk. I do not dare to say that he is such to God, for the Eternal Wisdom cannot be taken by surprise; yet the Eternal Wisdom requires me to say Yes or No and that is a mystery that I believe but cannot penetrate. However, certainly the Church takes a calculated risk. And in the light of the parables of the talents and the pounds, there is one thing you cannot do: you cannot play it safe. The money with which you traffic is not your own. To ask what is the integrity of a steward may perhaps find some answer by asking what is the discipline of that integrity.

I shall be able to speak only of one element in this discipline, and we may call it professional competence in handling the material used in preaching. I think that even the slight consideration of this which is here possible will open doors on other elements of the discipline and will reveal the nature of that integrity which we desire to possess. In this aspect the discipline is one of unremitting study. I believe that for the clergy today scarcely anything is more important. What? Are the clergy to become bookworms, to sit quietly in their libraries while the world burns and multitudes of people need their presence from one end of the city to the other and often from one end of the county to the other? I think there is very little danger of this. Everywhere one hears the same complaint, "I just can't get time to read." Perhaps some day after you leave the seminary you will say this, and it may be quite true that as your life has become organized there is too little time. Then, as the Navy says, Hear this! You'd better change the organization before it's too late. Now consider. On one of those afternoons when you are making ten calls, somebody comes up with precisely the solution to life that we heard from Bertrand Russell. What you had thought about it before, your understanding of the cultural influences that have produced it, your informed sympathy with the extent and depth of the human predicament before you, your intelligent grasp of those things that the man believes to be "quite beyond dispute," all this and a lot more that comes from reading, observation, and a well-nourished spiritual life determines your usefulness to the man before you. Will he find in you an experienced person capable of exploring his difficulties? The next person on your list that afternoon will be a woman whose husband has recently died. The next will be someone called a lapsed communicant, and this person, it now appears, is ablaze with a passion for social and international righteousness and utterly fed up with respectable Christianity. What are your calls for? What do you bring to them? What have you got time for?

Surely you must have time for that competence without which your ministrations are in vain: this competence comes from your studies in the seminary, and your continuing study, without which the seminary will have given you a Cook's tour of places you have seen but once. These places are Holy Scripture, Dogma, Liturgy, Moral Theology, Ascetic Theology. These delimit the area of your professional knowledge. Yet you are not dealing with them but with people; where the people are, your professional knowledge must acquire a double vocabulary: it must tell what the Word of God is and how to understand it; it must say what Christian belief is and why it ought to be believed; it must speak intelligently and lovingly about the worship of God; it must provide well-grounded and reasonable guidance for living with other people; it must teach people how to pray, how to use the sacraments, how to hold their souls before the living God. How much knowledge must you have, then, beyond your own special knowledge? Why, without doubt, as much as you can. Everything must be devoted in your pastoral and preaching ministry, not to the volume of service, but to the excellence of service. Therefore you must *know* the Bible, not merely know about it. You must be theologically literate. Many of us, I am sure, have heard sermons on the Holy Trinity that were purely Sabellian; perhaps we have heard some that were purely academic. Why should I believe in the Holy Trinity; there are many good Unitarians among my neighbors; what difference does it make? Is it sufficient to say that I must believe what the Church tells me to believe? Here surely is the supreme occasion to teach, to delight, and to move, on Trinity Sunday, that golden mountain-peak of the liturgical year! But must you invent the doctrine of the Trinity? Here then also is an occasion for theological competence. Nevertheless, the preacher must communicate to the people the Church's belief through his belief; he must communicate the Word of God through his own word. He must know it, he must believe it, he must live in it. Who is sufficient for this? You are, by the grace of God.

My reference to the doctrine of the Trinity has not been casual. On the contrary, I wish to dwell on it, and for three reasons: first, because it is central in the Christian belief in God; secondly, because with singular force it reveals both the demand and the difficulty of the preacher's task; and thirdly, because, if the doctrine is true, it cannot be without tremendous and wide-reaching implications for life.

First, then, is the doctrine. The doctrine is that "the Father is God, the Son is God, and the Holy Ghost is God, and yet there be not three Gods but one God." This is most indisputably the Catholic Faith and to it adhere, even in the present denominational confusion of the Christian movement, all but a very few of those who call themselves Christian. It confronts every man at his Baptism: with the invocation of the Name of God, the Father, the Son, and the Holy Ghost, I was named; and that, I suggest, means that my significance as a person, my very being as a person, is rooted in the Triune God; that whatever personality means in me is derived from the meaning of personality in God, and that I cannot be a person all by myself. Philosophically, the doctrine deals with the classical question of the One and the Many and proposes for it an ultimate resolution. In the theological quest for a suitable terminology, the Church was involved in the exploration of personality: in what way do the Biblical and human words, Father, Son, and Holy Spirit, refer to the eternal Being of the One and Only God? The Church does not say that there is no mystery of the Godhead beyond its own human language of definition, but it does believe that this mystery lies in the ultimate reality of that which is revealed in the New Testament and that the human words of this revelation, Father, Son, and Holy Spirit, are rightly and truly said concerning the Eternal God. For us Anglicans, this is indisputably *our* Faith as it is that of the whole Catholic Church of Christ. It is not a peripheral doctrine. It speaks of God, and in this language we speak *to* God. It is no metaphysical plaything for theologians. It is our religion.

In the second place, let us consider the demand and difficulty of the preacher's task in this regard. The demand is morally inescapable. That which the Church holds as its cardinal doctrine, namely the doctrine of God, that which dominates both the action and meaning of Holy Baptism, that which determines Christian prayer, which constitutes every benediction and as doxology concludes the Church's Eucharistic prayer, which informs the solemn Preface of the Eucharist on Trinity Sunday —that, I say, so mighty and so shining revelation may not be hidden under a shoddy bushel of careless or casual or merely occasional utterance. If it is to be believed by Christian people it must be not infrequently set before them as both necessary and worthy, and indeed, possible to be believed. Since the mystery of the Holy Trinity surpasses all human comprehension it surpasses all human utterance, but it does not forbid human utterance. To speak of God at all is to say what a man cannot say and yet to say that concerning which a man cannot keep silent. Apart from this the Christian preacher has nothing at all to say; and what he must say, what cries out within him for utterance, he will find, with the help of God, a way to utter. There is nothing human of which a preacher may not speak and there is nothing human of which he may speak without reference to God. The task of the preacher is defined not only by the truth of God but by the people's need to know that truth. What truth? Is the Trinity true, or is it a venerable and ancient declaration for optional subscription? I commend to you the robust assertion of John Donne:

> The first, and principal duty of him, who in-
> grafted himself into the body of the Christian
> Church, by Baptism, is to inform himself of the
> Trinity, in whose Name he is baptized.

Upon this assumption, he defines further the stages
of this informing: What the doctrine is; how we
are to learn and understand it; and how far we
should search into this mystery.

Here the difficulty of the preacher's task meets us.
The doctrine must first of all be accurately declared.
This is not effected by quoting the Church's formularies, for it must be illustrated by the aberrations
from which the formularies seek to guard us. I am
sure you will discover that these aberrations are
as mischievous today as they were formerly, notwithstanding the modern terms in which they find
expression. Your theological education prepares you
for this. I would urge you especially to understand
the ancient heresies as alternative possibilities of in-
terpreting the Christian Faith and of confronting
the revelation of God in Israel, in His Only-Begotten Son and in the Christian community's apprehension of its own life in the Spirit; and to consider as
well that the statement of the Church's Faith in this

regard, which required some centuries of exploration, is an exploration of personality and of the divine disclosure made in Christ. It is always the exploration of Holy Scripture and of the revelation there related as it constitutes and is apprehended within the Christian community.

You must consider, too, with what preconceptions people hear your presentation of Christian doctrine. In this Church, as a recent survey has shown, the people believe more generally and personally in the Trinity than we might have feared, though I suspect that the liturgy with little assistance from the pulpit is responsible for this. But they are not unaffected by environing influences. I venture to suggest that there are always three possible apprehensions of the divine pluralism: "gods many and lords many"; monism, where however the divine is construed, it is never construed through personality and is never a moral confrontation; and the Hebrew belief in the Living God, the One and Only, transcendent and sovereign. Out of the last of these three arises the doctrine of the Trinity, but apart from that arising, as Islam discloses, the belief shrivels, as it unmistakably does in the modern Christian world, to a mere Unitarianism, the ascription of personality to a monad. For many Christians, I fear, God is exclusively the Father, Christ His divine representation in humanity, and the Holy Spirit a benign influence or emanation from God. With this, or with a confused monism, your preaching is met, and it is this you must overcome.

You cannot do this with philosophy alone, nor yet alone with Christian formularies. Here again there is work for the imagination. Man is ineradicably mythopoetic, and only by the tricks of sophisticated abstraction can he be made to think that the I—Thou—We of his own experience can be answered by nothing more than a cosmic It. He says, Tell me a story, and God gives him the story of the eternal love within the Godhead, active in Creation and in Redemption, in the human language and the human action of Christ. So, notwithstanding all the ineptitudes and dangers of analogy and similitude, we are encouraged by Holy Scripture, and not least of all by our Lord's example, to speak even of the deepest things of God with imagery, with human warmth and color, and thus to speak to the

heart no less than to the mind. Let me quote to you
something from the volume of Negro sermons by
James Johnson called *God's Trombones*.

And God stepped out on space,
And He looked around and said:
I'm lonely—
I'll make me a world.
And far as the eye of God could see
Darkness covered everything,
Blacker than a hundred midnights
Down in a cypress swamp.
And God smiled,
And the light broke,
And the darkness rolled up on one side,
And the light stood shining on the other,
And God said: That's good!

Then God reached out and took the light in his hands
And God rolled the light around in his hands
Until he made the sun;
And he set that sun a-blazing in the heavens.
And the light that was left over from making the sun
God gathered it up in a shining ball
And flung it against the darkness,
Spangling the night with the moon and stars.
Then down between
The darkness and the light

He hurled the world;
And God said: That's good! [3]

I am sorry I cannot quote more of this; and I am more sorry still that I must find fault with so moving a composition. Yet I must, for it is wrong if it proposes to speak of Creation in a Christian voice. The Creation springs from the love that is eternally rejoiced within the Trinity, and not from the loneliness of God. God sitting up lonesome on His golden throne and casting about for something or someone to love is not the Christian story.

The Christian story is that the Creation is the work of divine love and of divine joy. It is not for the consolation of God's solitariness; it is not the antidote to a self-preoccupied paranoia in excelsis; it is not the means of self-realization for an otherwise unexpressed Being. The God in whom Christians believe is within Himself perfect and needing nothing, yet needing nothing because within the Divine Being there is that ultimate reality of personal relationship, of mutual self-giving and rejoicing in one another, which gives to love its meaning.

[3] James Johnson, "The Creation," *God's Trombones*. The Viking Press, 1927.

If this is anthropomorphic, let us not cringe, for whoever would speak of love is speaking anthropomorphically. Indeed, whenever a man speaks he speaks as a man. If he says there is no God, he says that behind phenomena there is no He or They, but merely the cause It or the fact It: and *It*, if it refers to a postulated Nothing, means nothing; and if it is taken from human experience and vocabulary, as indeed it is, is much less than Thou and I and We. Christianity asserts that love is at the beginning of all, and over all, and at the end of all—love that can be given and known and given in return, because that is what God is.

Now in our experience there is one intimation, and that most sacred to Christians, of how Creation can be conceived as a sovereign work of love, and that is the birth of a child. This is only an intimation, because no creature can create except, so to speak, by imitation and with derived creativeness; and, moreover, in no creature and in no society of creatures is there any sovereign self-sufficiency. Yet since marriage is a mirror of the mystical unity between Christ and His Church, and because in God every Fatherhood is named, we may perceive how from a fullness of given and requited love, rather than from an emptiness and need of love, a new life comes to be. This is in the successiveness of man, within the flow of time, a reflection in the moving water of man's creaturehood.

As an intimation it must not be pushed to mean that the Creation is of the substance of deity. What it does mean is that man is made in the image of God as personality in relationship; that the family, and society in its perfection, is an image of deity; and through it, also, something beyond a merely metaphysical meaning is given to the doctrine of the Trinity. Yet we must be cautious in using the family metaphor. Perhaps you have heard, as I have, explanations which try to draw an exact parallel with an earthly family by ascribing a kind of maternity to the Holy Spirit. This is quite inadmissible, and wherever anything of this kind has appeared in Christianity it has opened the door to ancient and mischievous tendencies arising out of primitive religion. What the Church has understood in the Scriptural revelation is that the fountain and origin of divine Being is in the Father; that the Son, because he is eternally Son, is eternally begotten; and that the Holy Spirit eternally proceeds from the Father. The Western "double procession," whatever be its defense, certainly cannot be made to mean that there are two sources of divine Being.

Since this governs our belief and governs our prayer it must also in some striving for expression govern our preaching if that preaching is to be thoroughly and definitively Christian. The Christian story which enshrines it is already given. We do not need to invent it for ourselves. What we need is to be conscious of it in its epic grandeur; to be ourselves the enchanted and ever-wondering hearers of it and the inspired tellers of it, the minstrels of God's poem. At the dawning, at the beginning, One stood on the threshold between being and becoming. He stood surrounded and enfolded by light, and when He spoke it was as though He listened for what He said. The Word which He uttered was not only His own, as He stood not alone, but stood to utter and to do the command that came from within the serene effulgence which He shared. And within the same effulgence was also another movement, alive and stirring in the same serenity, like the movement of the air on a night of stars in the mountains, alive and deeply felt as though it neither comes nor goes, but is simply there, moving. When He spoke, over across the threshold, in what had been nothing, there was another, a different light, as when the rising sun makes the western sky aflame with reflected color and out of the void of the night's darkness awakes to life the manifold Something of all creatures. He Himself was the Word He spoke, as a man's speech is the revelation of a man. His Word was the execution of His Father's Will, that He should make that which within the Counsel of the Godhead had been determined to be made. By a majestic working He entered into the Something of incalculable myriads as it were of sparks, and by an operation of incomparable intellectual grandeur, gathered them into millions of blazing suns, and appointed for a thousand thousand galaxies their interactive motions. What He has done or is doing with these man does not know; and even though man should fly to them and tread upon them man could not know the meaning of God's work in them unless first he learned aright the meaning of God's work here. But if man could stand upon the barren and awful planets that surround him, and gaze upon the earth given to him, he would see of a truth how lovely a garden God has planted for him. For here are in profusion the signs of the working of the Eternal Word: out of the lowest intimations of life, out of the slime of the earth, has moved a procession of forms in which the wisdom and providence of God is seen in a rolling system of interdependent life striving upwards for its consummation. The very trees uphold the hills to which they cling, and from the upward march of creatures has come one of themselves whose nature can be taken by the Eternal Word who made it.

But when this has become possible, something else also has become possible. The nature that can say Yes to God can say No. What hath God wrought? In all heresy there seems to me to be some common shrinking from any real contact of God with creation and sin, whether by its possibility in His Creation or by any genuine action on His part in redemption. Perhaps in some way this is due to a failure to recognize that the mediatorial work of Christ is imbedded in His eternal

Nature as the Word. His contact with the creature, and so to speak His responsibility for the creature, does not begin with the Incarnation. As for man himself, God did not choose a robot for His gardener, nor a slave for His priest, nor a mechanical doll for a son adopted in the Beloved.

From the dawning when He stepped upon that threshold whence all things become, He who executes the counsel of the Blessed Trinity has planted a garden for a gardener, has made a universe to be offered by a priest, has built a City for sons who shall serve with freedom. For such a work, redemption is no afterthought. Look then on this picture: Lucifer, standing near the Throne, a shining prince of creatures, enviously desires to be as God, though it is impossible—if we may say so reverently, not possibly within the gift of God to any creature. But the desire for it is possible for whom free submission is possible. Envy and frustration devour him until he falls from the place he has come to hate; and being self-devoured he falls down to devour, to deceive, to destroy. Now behold Him who, since He is God, is so by no rapacity, as St. Paul says. For love He came down, by His own will, and took upon Himself the form of a servant that He might with His own dear life be the food of servants. Evil is always a devouring and a destroying, and good is always a feeding and an exalting.

There is then another picture: Imagine yourself in a theatre, utterly dark save for an incredible beauty of light and movement on the stage. From a Throne there moves a radiant Figure, down through ranks of angels hushed in wonder, towards a golden gate at the proscenium. The gate opens; He steps forth—and on the instant the house lights swell, the stage is hidden by a curtain in darkness, and before you, amongst you, is a little Child in the arms of a human mother. As a child, as a young man, He grows in wisdom and stature, and in favor with God and man. When men cry to God from their struggles and their miseries, saying, "You, there on your golden throne, what do you know and what do you care for us and our life!" there comes from among themselves a voice saying, "I know and I care for I am one of you." He has come working, as He said, "My Father worketh hitherto and I work." He has come to build a Temple, to make a living Body of Mankind, to win and claim a Bride. For this He died, for this He rose, that in all we might be with Him as He has been with us.

I gave you three reasons for dwelling on the doctrine of the Trinity. The last of them, its manifold relevance, is the reason also for dwelling on it in this lecture. The revolutionary and chaotic age we live in has raised for men everywhere with singular urgency a question which is distinctly eschatological. It is a question about the meaning of existence, for man in the vast cosmic movement, for man in relation to his own society, for each man in his own life. This is not a new question, for it is always man's question, and it is always inescapably eschatological. But now the eschatological heart of the question beats loudly in our ears, not so much as the meaning of the end as the end that is in the meaning. Is man's life, any man's life, and is human society, human history, human destiny, of any more account in the universe than a hydrogen flame on the surface of the sun? Bertrand Russell, in the passage I have quoted, uses the phrase, "the whole temple of man's achievement." This is a great thought, that all human achievement is the place where man meets his God. But what God meets him there? If it is only, as in Lafcadio Hearn's story of the Japanese shrine, the reflection of his own face in a mirror, then man at his noblest becomes the God that ought to have been but never was, lying, as though he had never been, in the debris of a universe in ruins. This is indeed a desperate faith. Let us go down grandly, with our colors tattered but still aloft, for there is neither in the sea beneath nor in the sky above anyone who cares.

Perhaps this is a faith for dying, but it is not a good one for living. If you want to live grandly, what is grand, and why is it so? Suppose I do not want to live grandly; I want to get what I can and the devil take the hindmost, as the elephant said when he danced among the chickens. Why should I not? Because it is bad for society? But why is Nietzsche wrong, why should the strong not rule as they will? Is there in the universe any sanction to the contrary? In many places in the world today society crushes with its dragon-tail all human freedom and all personal rights because for that society there are no sanctions to the contrary. There is nothing that man can make more cruelly hostile to what, in the humanist twilight of Christianity, are mildly called "human values," than a society that has become its own reason for being.

But it is a false antithesis, whether man exists for society or society for man. Man is not possible apart from society, and society is infra-human apart from the human dignity and freedom of its members. In society man seeks in the family, in friendship, and in the civil and religious community, the way to be most fully himself. This human community, certainly ever since the domestication of animals, has included other species than himself; it includes flowers and green grass no less than grain and fruit trees; with other men he scans the heavens and scrutinizes the rocks and the oceans, as scientist and as poet; and in all he rises to be most truly himself as a lover rather than a user. All depredation upon natural resources, all inhumanity to animals, all exploitations of man by man come from using without love and without reverence. The perennial quest of man in the state he builds is for some way of living in freedom under rightful authority. His quest is for justice, which means nothing except in the relationship of persons. Is justice rooted in God, or is it only a device for the internal government of the human race? Is love but a phenomenon of creatures, or is it, perfectly, supremely, and in a manner of which all human love is but an obscure mirror, within the Godhead, a Unity of free giving and requital pouring forth out of its eternal fullness into creation, into redemption, into a working that on the day of its finishing will be good as the beginning was good? Is this not what you must speak about in a time of troubles, or indeed, in any time?

Lecture 4

PRIESTHOOD AND THE WORD

THE SUBJECT of this lecture, "Priesthood and the Word," obliges us to explore the nature and function of the Christian ministry. It is a well-worn theme and will doubtless be debated till the Lord comes again. It is a work for specialists in the Holy Scriptures, in dogmatic theology, in history and in liturgiology, and its exploration requires of us reference to them and deference to them. It also requires the gathering together of their researches and their conclusions. This would employ a learning so versatile and a mind so judicious that few men are capable of it on a grand scale. Still, there have been and there are such men; yet we find among them—to put it modestly—a number of minor disagreements which drive us to do some thinking for ourselves. But why? Shall we not be satisfied, if we are Catholics, with what the Church teaches, or, if we are Protestants, with what the Bible teaches? No, not until we know what the Church and the Bible really teach.

This is why we must explore for ourselves, not only to find out what is true, but to penetrate its significance. To do this, to think about the meaning of the Christian ministry, carries us into the deepest recesses of the Christian Faith. This becomes for us an even more solemn obligation because we are sent to teach others, so that they too, with our maps and with such guiding as one man can give to another, may explore for themselves the deep things of Christ. The Church cannot use parrots for its teachers, but if it could they are cheaper to educate than men and can repeat what they are taught with no danger of private interpretation.

In order to speak of the ministry, we must begin with the Person and work of Christ, since it is therefrom that the Church, and the ministry within it, derive what they are and what they do.

You will doubtless have noticed that there are four categorical designations of our Lord in the New Testament: Son, Word, Priest, and King. He is the Son of Man and the Son of God. He is the Word of God who is with God and who is God.

He is the Priest forever, and correlative with that, the Lamb slain from the foundation of the world.[1] He is the King, the Messiah, anointed by the Holy Spirit. You will have noted also that these are all designations of agency, indicating derivation, responsibility, and obedience. The idea of a son is totally meaningless apart from a father, and our Lord constantly declares His obedience. He is the Word of the Father. A priest is the minister of another than himself. Both priest and king must have anointing, in the Old Testament. The Father has appointed Him a Kingdom and He must reign until all enemies shall be subdued, and then the Kingdom shall be rendered up to the Father.

But these are designations which transcend his-

[1] Rev. 13:8. The translation is uncertain. The A.R.S.V., following the A.S.V. of 1901, reads "written before the foundation of the world." The English revision agrees with the A.V., "slain from the foundation of the world." In the Greek, as Ernst Lohmeyer remarks (*Die Offenbarung des Johannes*, 2nd. ed., Tubingen, 1953, p. 112), the latter translation has the advantage place-wise; but the true parallel is in 17:8, which affords strong confirmation of the former. The essential consideration, however, is that the book is the book of the Lamb slaughtered in sacrifice. The governing passage is in chap. 5. The Lamb is emblazoned with the emblems of the Holy Ghost, the seven horns of might and seven eyes of omniscience. In this passage the Lamb has cosmic centrality and holds the book of eternal destiny because His redeeming death in sacrifice is the act of an eternal Redeemer.

tory. They are not applied merely to a man called Jesus, or merely in relation to His destiny as to one who should be born. They are applied to a nature and an activity within the Godhead which is never absent from the world and from history but which in the one historic coming, in the one human life, makes the revelation and does the deed. The revelation is the glory of God and the deed is the glorification of God. But what reveals and does is not just a nature and activity, a universal abstraction, a concept for philosophers. Not at all. Jesus reveals, Jesus does the mighty deed. But unless He is Emmanuel, God truly with us, what can He reveal and what can He do?—only the pathetic illusion, only the ultimate gallant gesture of man standing before the black curtain of the enigma; the God who ought to be if only He were. But in Jesus the fullness of the Godhead dwelt bodily so that we can see the glory of God in His face. Through His perfect filial piety shone the eternal Sonship. His human speech was the speaking of the Divine Word. By His dying, His rising again, and His Ascension into the Place of the Holy, that is to say, the Place not made here, He made and eternally makes the one, the cosmic offering. He came to claim the Kingdom that belongs to Him, and in Him, the Kingdom came.

This was by a real Incarnation, in manhood up to the hilt, to be as dead as a man can be. No wonder that it arouses such faith and provokes such incredulity. This may seem strange to us who are Christians, yet it is true that men find it easier to believe in a divine apparition or in the doctrines of a human prophet than to believe in the Incarnation. Even Christians find it hard to believe. The history of the Ecumenical Councils shows that this is so, and I think it is equally evident in many modern expressions that are substantially Monophysitic, Sabellian, or Adoptianist. The invasion of Hellenism has been so much charged with producing the Nicene Faith that I cannot forbear to remind you of what a thoroughgoing Hellenist said about it. The Emperor Julian said that "it was this John who, by declaring that the Word was made flesh, wrought all the mischief." Well, if Christianity is mischief, Julian put his finger on the cause of it, though John is not alone to be blamed for it. Things equally bold are said in the opening sentence of Mark's Gospel; in the opening verses of Hebrews; in the second chapter of Philippians; in I Timothy 3:16; in Ephesians 1:10. In this last citation is one of the boldest statements of the New Testament, for it asserts that it is God's purpose to gather up in Christ the whole creation. Over and over in the New Testament we find an eschatology that is cosmic: the whole creation moves to the consummation of God's creating act, and not to its defeat. Redemption, therefore, is not the afterthought of a God compelled by the emergence of evil to devise a new plan. Only a second-rate God would be so conceived.

To say that Jesus has "cosmic significance" is not enough. Everything has cosmic significance that is in the cosmos. The personal pronoun "He" is used in the New Testament no less than in the Nicene Creed with a continuous identity to denote the Maker of the world, the Man, Christ Jesus, who died and rose and ascended, and the Victor enthroned now "far above all the heavens that He might fill all things." But God made the world; God was in Christ, reconciling the world unto Himself; and the consummation of all things is that God "may be all in all." It was the conviction of the first Christians that as man did not make the world and himself in it, so no man who is no more than a man can save the world and himself in it. They believed that all men have sinned and that all men need redemption. But they did not believe that this Man needed redemption, and they did believe that He was the Saviour of the world. They believed that God was in Him in a supreme action of reconciliation and that salvation is in the Blood of Jesus. They believed that although all things were created in Him, He became flesh and was obedient even unto death. The terms they applied to Him—Son, Word, Priest, King—faithfully reflected their remembrance of His disclosure to them of His own self-consciousness. His life was one of perfect obedience; the Word He spoke was not His but His Father's; He declared His death to be an offering for the sin of the world, and His Blood the Blood of the Covenant; and the Kingdom of God, which He came to proclaim, He believed had been appointed to Him as its King by the Father. You cannot make the New Testament say that the God and Father of our Lord Jesus Christ died and rose and ascended to the right hand of the Majesty on high.

It is plain, then, that our Lord's incarnate life is a ministry. It was so described by the terms of agency applied to Him, and it was so in fact by His words and by His deeds. Moreover, since we do not speak of the Incarnation as something only in the past, the Incarnation is now and it will be forever. There is something here that surpasses the conception and the speech of man: man has a word for it, but what the word means he does not know. It is the word *eternity*. For people accustomed to big words, it may be called an intimation fugitive but persistent that, to use Von Hugel's phrase, englobes the simultaneity of God in the successiveness of man. But other people have it who are not articulate in that way, perhaps not articulate at all; millions of them, and I think all men do, for the word "eternity" is common, and when it appears in a movie title, all the people in the theatre feel a familiar meaning though they cannot at all define it. When you stand on the deck of a ship at night with the great sea rolling under you, it does not seem strange to think that you and the ship and the sea and all things and all time float on something other, timeless but real. Does not the Incarnation speak of this? It has moral meaning of course, because it brings salvation from sin. But the word *moral* can be, and often is, so restricted in its implications that it does not reach into the depths of personality where the self hungers for union and for vision. As I stand by the ship's rail and know that what happens to the ship and to all of us who are in it makes no difference whatever to the sea, I wonder whether eternity is like that. What will it matter when everything is finished? Will anything really have occurred? For this, the Incarnation is the all-sufficient reassurance. It testifies that what has been and what has not been do not in the end come to the same thing. There was a time when Christ was not man, and for all time hereafter He is man. Yet He spans all time, for He spoke the Word of Creation at the beginning, and the Manhood which He took in time reigns in eternity.

Far from being merely metaphysical and unimaginable, eternity is experienced as a transfiguration of ordinary and temporal life, and it is imaginable as the attainment of real life in the present tense. It is ever-lasting time that is unimaginable, for in its endless succession there can be no consummation but only an infinite becoming. For the human spirit this is intolerable. We seek an abiding city, but in time all cities lie, and must lie, level upon level, like the ruins of Jericho, each rising from the debris of those that were before. In time the present forever eludes us, flowing inexorably away. Can you think of it, and if you can, does it not appall you—to live forever in the never-ending regress of the present into the ir-recoverable past? The Gospel has something better for us than this. In the homeliest and simplest words, He has spoken to us of a *harvesting*. That speaks to us of consummation, and it is not unimaginable.

Christ's ministry is not circumscribed by His earthly life, for it continues to the end of time: "He ever liveth to make intercession." But did it begin with His earthly life? Do the terms of agency and ministry apply only to His Manhood? Did they arise out of the Incarnation? You know that the Church does not believe this. You know that the Sonship which is expressed in His human filial piety is the ex-pression of His Eternal Sonship; that He spoke the

Father's Word because He is the Father's Word, uttered at the beginning from within the Godhead; you know that what He did on Calvary and declared at the institution of the Eucharist is the eternal offering of an eternal Priest; and that His everlasting Kingdom is the Kingdom of His Father. These things so inform the liturgy and the other offices of the Church, and not least, the great hymns of Christianity, that we must say them and sing them, not once or twice, but over and over in all our worship. They say that the ministry of Christ projects into history, into historical doing, something that is eternal within the Godhead.

This becomes clearer when you consider that this ministry is not, so to speak, in the first place directed towards man but rather towards God. He came to fulfill the Law and the Prophets, He came to do the Father's Will, He came to give His life a ransom for many—and here I must remind you that this word *ransom* is used in the First Epistle of Peter in the context of sacrifice. His work was to glorify the Father. His work towards man is one of compassion, of reproof, of teaching, of consolation, of never-failing love, to bring men to the Father. Through the action of the Son the Father is revealed and His work is accomplished. Through ministering a man can reveal God and do God's work, as you are preparing to do. But your ministry is derived, it is given to you from Christ, it is His ministry in you and yet it is yours. Christ's ministry was not derived, and certainly not from Aaron, yet it was *a ministry proper to man and reveals the true meaning of manhood*. It is proper to man to glorify God, to speak God's truth as it shall be given to him, to offer himself to God and help others to do the same, to live in filial obedience to God and help others to do the same, to rule his own life as God's servant and help others to do the same. But the act of ministering, *the being a minister, the directing the totality of ministering towards God*, does not reveal what God *is* unless it expresses something *in* God: for the essence of ministry is offering to God.

This is what we must now consider, but particularly with reference to the relation between priesthood and the Word.

One could scarcely miss, in the Prologue of St. John, an echo of the opening verses of Genesis. In the beginning God said. . . . In the beginning was the Word. In Christ, the Word of Creation reaches its destination in evoking in Creation an Image of God. He who is in His Deity the Image of God enters into Creation and makes real in man, by the actual life of man, the full human destiny. The Father did not become man, and yet the Son did not do it, as our fumbling human minds oblige us to say it, all by Himself. Theology, in order to say neither that there are three Gods nor that there is only one actor playing three roles, endeavors to speak about a coinherence of the Trinity; yet it comes inevitably to a kind of ontological stammering, as when Tertullian says *"tres personae unum sunt."* The Three Persons are one—what? But what Christian Faith says is not said with an eye to philosophy. What it says is at once positive and naïve, and it cannot allow what it says to be irrevocably committed to any philosophical idiom, though it is obliged, in the apologetic which is a subsequent activity of faith, to use philosophy as a language. But at any cost, it must speak its mind and let the philosophical chips fall where they will. Do not lament Christian naïveté, but rather glory in it. When Plotinus died, he said, "Now that which is divine in me is reunited to what is divine in the universe"; but when Jesus died, He said, "Father, into Thy hands I commend my spirit." The Son came seeking us because the Father sent Him: "I say not that I will pray the Father for you, for the Father Himself loveth you." When Jesus was baptized, the Holy Spirit came upon Him and the Father's Voice called Him the Beloved Son. Here is essentially the Christian thing, the thing that we must say in whatever philosophy, for the loftiest and deepest things in the New Testament are in narrative and in picture: in them is the true and shining meaning of the Revelation in Jesus of the true and shining Name of God, the Father, the Son, and the Holy Ghost.

Christ, then, is the Father's Word spoken at Creation. In His historical coming, He spoke the Word of Redemption, and this too is the Father's Word. Are they then *two* words? We have already declined to think of redemption as God's afterthought, the provision of a kind of alternative landing-field because Creation had gone off its course. Christ is in Himself the *one Word*. I think you see this more clearly when you recognize that St. John's Prologue is not completed at the fourteenth verse but at the eighteenth: "In the beginning was the Word . . . All things were made by him . . . and the Word was made flesh . . . no man hath seen God at any time; the only begotten Son, which is in the bosom of the Father, he hath declared him." The word translated "declared" is the word from which we get exegesis: it means to expound, to declare the meaning. In Christ the meaning of the Word at Creation is expounded. He became flesh, and in that flesh which our eyes have seen and our hands have handled, we have beheld the glory of God, full of truth and grace. And the glory shines full and clear in the lifting up of the Son of Man upon the Cross. Thus in Redemption the Word of Creation becomes the Word of creating-anew, of *regeneration*. To all who receive Him, He gives the power to become what they were created to be, the sons of God by grace. This is the Father's Will which is brought to living effectuality not only by the power and gift of the Son but by the new birth in the Holy Spirit. Hereby is the destiny of Creation accomplished: not in another man but in a new man, in the trans-formation of man and the transfiguration of the world awaiting the gathering-up of all things in Christ.

Christ, who is the Word of Redemption, spoke

the Word of Redemption. The evidence of His Mission, as He sent it back to John in prison, is the evidence of restoration: the blind receive their sight and the lame walk. This is no mere "concept" of restoration; these are individual people: they were blind, and are no longer blind. There is a justifiable impatience of Christianity. It is not justified when we do not succeed in doing what we say: for that, as for the Disciples with the epileptic boy, more penitence and prayer are needed. It is justified, however, when it does not appear that we desire and intend to do what we say. The Christian Church is at once the society of the redeemed and the redeeming society. This is important to be said here, though we must come back to it later. But I do want to remind you here that the releasing and restoring work of our Lord is a releasing of men and women from bondage and a restoring them to the service of God so that they may be an offering to Him. To restore all things in Christ is the purpose of Redemption. To whom are they restored? To themselves, or to God? Is not the one a step to the other?

But the climactic, the supremely unequivocal Word of Redemption was spoken at the Last Sup-

per. There, more than anywhere else, is revealed the
Lord's own interpretation of His death. He declares
that by His own sovereign disposal of Himself, He
is making the Offering of the Covenant. In Geth-
semane He offers His will, and on Calvary He
offers His Body. "It is this consecrating word," as
Sir Edwyn Hoskyns says, "and not the murderous
activity of the Jews, that makes His death an effective and redemptive act.[2] To this the Synoptic tradition and St. Paul bear witness, and in the Fourth
Gospel it receives a peculiar emphasis from the omission of the Words of Institution from the narrative
of the Upper Room. It is hard to resist the impression that the omission is deliberate, yet not at all
either through ignorance of the Institution narrative
or through repudiation of it. On the contrary, although the little homily on eating His Flesh and
drinking His Blood closely follows the Feeding of
the Five Thousand, the drinking of blood has no
relevance to that event and must be clearly derived,
and accepted, from the general tradition of the
Church: for if there is a *hard* saying, in this reference

[2] *The Fourth Gospel,* by Sir Edwyn Hoskyns, edited by F. N. Da-
vey. Faber and Faber, 1940. Vol. II, p. 596.

to Flesh and Blood, it is the Marcan saying, and, earlier than that, the Pauline. In the Upper Room narrative, St. John's Gospel concentrates attention, not on the blessing and distribution of the Bread and the Cup, but on the Lord's Word of sanctifying and offering Himself to the Father, and the Church in Him. It is this Word, and it is spoken in prayer, that gives the Bread and the Cup their meaning and their efficacy.

Here is revealed the conjunction of priesthood and the Word. By His Word of priesthood and offering, our Lord sanctified His death as a sacrifice to fulfill the Father's Will for the redemption of the world. By His Word He declared to His Disciples that this was the meaning of His death. By His Word upon the Bread and upon the Cup, He gives Himself to them, and to all who shall believe on Him through their word, to become *their* offering, so that in union with Him, they may become a reasonable, holy, and living sacrifice to the Father in joy and in gladness. If the Eucharist were no more than a bare remembrance of the Upper Room, it could not be a remembering of anything less or other than this; and if, loving Jesus and believing in

Him, we were only to remember, how could we remember without accepting Him as our offering, and how could we accept without offering? Beneath mountains of controversy and after centuries of altercation, I cannot but believe that this lies, in some way through the grace of God, ready to be awakened in the hearts of Christians everywhere in a majestic unison of Eucharistic life. We have no offering but Christ, and no priesthood but His. If He had not made Himself the Oblation, we could not offer Him, yet only by offering Him can we truly accept Him as our Oblation. If we are His Body, we are united with Him in His priesthood and in His offering: if we are the Temple of God, as St. Paul says we are, we are the place of that offering, a *thusiasterion*, a place of sacrifice, as St. Ignatius of Antioch calls the Church.

Now a priest must say words. He must pray the liturgy in which by words the action is offered through prayer to God, and in which likewise by words the meaning of what is done is declared in the hearing of men, of angels and archangels, and all the company of Heaven. For this there is no stopping, from the words of the liturgy at the altar to the proclamation of the Gospel in the hearing of men to the uttermost parts of the earth. We are sent to baptize and to teach. We are sent with words to draw all men who will come into the fellowship of the mystery so that they may pray to the true and living God and with their understanding be made partakers of the brotherhood of Christ. The word and the act must be inseparable, from the altar to the market, because they are inseparable in Him who as Son of God and Son of Man is Word and Priest and King.

And now, through the consideration of Christ's ministry we are come to the consideration of our own. By "our own" I mean that of the Church herself, for the ministry in Holy Orders is what it is because of Christ and the Church.

Need we ask whether the ministry of Christ is communicable? We should not need to, if there had not been a long controversy about priesthood. This controversy has in our time reached the unhappy stage where it becomes necessary to debate even that the idea of priesthood is genuinely involved in a valid Christology. It was certainly involved in the Christology of the New Testament.

This of course raises for the modern mind the question, What did Jesus think about Himself? Historically this is impossible to determine independently of the New Testament. Within those documents, study and inquiry must have the right to move freely, because Christianity is a historical religion which asserts that its whole life is drawn from its origin. *Within* these documents and *upon* them discussion has a right to flourish, but it will flourish only so long as Christianity is a living religion, and when all is said it will be of interest to few who are not Christians. But there is no way of escaping *from those documents.* The patristic Church astutely perceived that there is no possible way of identifying or verifying the Christian Gospel *apart* from the documents which constitute the Canon set up by the Church for the identification of herself. In plain terms, this means that there is no way of recognizing Jesus except through the eyes of His Apostles and Disciples and through the writings produced in the communities which they founded.

Well, then, in the New Testament the ministry of Christ is communicable, and under precisely the same figures by which the ministry of Christ is understood. It becomes the ministry of the Church. We are the sons of God by adoption and grace. We are sent to speak the Word of Redemption in Baptism by water and the Spirit, and to expound the meaning of Redemption in Christian teaching. By the Lamb we have been made a priesthood and a Kingdom unto our God. In all this, like the prophets at Antioch, we minister *unto the Lord;* the whole life of the Church is to be an extension, through the ministry of every member in his own vocation, of the liturgy, an action of worship. When Christians forget this, either their lives fall away from their worship or their worship falls away and dies out of their living.

Clearly there is in the New Testament a doctrine of the universal priesthood of all believers who by Baptism have entered into the *Koinonia.* But it is grotesque to call it the priesthood only of the laity. Such a phrase carries the absurdity that though Christ is a priest and His people a priesthood, His ministers are not.

But what is the *Laos?* It is not the *hoi polloi,* if you like a Greek remark, or the vulgar *plebs* if you prefer a Latin word. It is the People of God, the

ecclesia, the called-out. This is a Biblical idea and it
enters Christianity from the Old Testament. The
Church is not another Israel: it is the *new* Israel. Is
there a more natural reason for the Twelve, the
Patriarchs of the New Israel who shall sit on twelve
thrones judging the tribes, or for the vision of the
twenty-four Elders, before God's Throne, repre-
senting the full and true Israel, or for the twelve
Foundations of the City of God? Observe the way
in which the Gospel approaches a universal brotherhood of man. It does not abolish the sacred people
and dissolve it into the secular order, into "the
nations." On the contrary, it breaks down the wall
of partition between Jew and Gentile by offering
to all men on the sole condition of belief and Baptism admission into the sacred brotherhood. This,
says St. Paul, is the great mystery, revealed by the
Holy Spirit, that the Gentiles should be fellow-heirs
and of the same Body. In ways beyond our knowing,
this extends backward to the creation of man, for
Christ died not only for those who should live after
His Incarnation. In the words of St. Gregory the
Great, "The saints before the Law, the saints under
the Law, and the saints under grace, all these making

up the Lord's Body, were constituted members of the Church." There is indeed a radical Christian laicism which demands a harder thing than preaching the Gospel in the secular world. It demands the Christian invasion of the secular world by the opening of the way to God's altar without respect to race or class through inclusion of any man or woman to the life of the Brotherhood on no other terms than those of Jesus. Every man is not a layman, but every man is a *potential* layman; every layman is not potentially a priest for every layman is a priest. Can a layman speak the Word? Can a layman offer the Eucharist? *In the Church he can and he does.* What do the laity come to the Eucharist for—only to receive Holy Communion? What is the Liturgical Action if not the Action of the Church—the Action within the Church of the Lord Himself!

But God hath set in the Church a ministry. We have no concern in this discussion for exploring how the rich and varied ministry in the New Testament settled down into the hierarchy of Holy Orders. It did happen rapidly and left no scars of protestation, and this Order of the Church stands not only in the Great Tradition but in the allegiance of the large majority of all Christians today. The Ignatian Epistles do not prove that it was universal when they were written but they deserve something better than the rather patronizing dismissal they receive from some writers who seem to regard their author as a neurotic episcopo-maniac. And before the end of the first century, was Clement inventing some newfangled clericalism to throw gasoline on the fire at Corinth when he reminded the Corinthians that "the Apostles had provided a continuance"? Nevertheless, as I say, this is not our inquiry. What concerns us is only that the ministry *in* the Church is the ministry *of* the Church, set there as a function of the Body by the Lord. This is illuminated in the principle of ordination, for in ordination there is, so to speak, a double motion. Through history the ministry devolves by succession, by the laying-on of the Bishop's hands, and in both orders above the Diaconate, with others of the same order as that which is being given. But there is also a direct and vertical movement, from God immediately, on him who is called, tried, and examined before the Brethren. The *Veni Creator Spiritus* is sung, and this is prayer for the direct, immediate action of God.

These two motions come together in the Act of Ordaining, and both are from God, His single Action by His promise and by His power.

Does this annul the priesthood of the Church? Does succession from the Apostles operating in explicit petition to God lower the state and dignity of God's people? Alas, it can appear to do so in every sort of corruption of the Church. Yet would it be more noble if those who must inevitably perform some service of ministering among the brethren were commissioned only, were only distinguished by qualifications of character and training? If there were any prayer at all, if it asked anything directly of God, such a view would dismiss ordination through the door only to admit the shadow of it through the window. But the essential question is, What does the ministry do? It does what Christ does in and through His Church. It is a ministry of the sacraments and of the Word because He who is Priest is Word. There is a power of offering and of preaching in the Christian priesthood which belongs to ordination not for tearing down but for building up, not *instead* of the Church, but *within* the Church.

To this "weighty Office and Charge" you are called. It presents an image of the ministry beautiful to contemplate but one which becomes substantial in the homes of people, in the turbulence of cities, in the dust of the comon road. Here the Gospel must be declared, here it must be given its exegesis. The tool of the ministry is language, and its business is communication. In administering sacraments the priest must enunciate language, and in teaching how to use them he must communicate their meaning. In everything he must be a man proficient with words. In every parish you meet problems of communication, and in some, as Father Myers has been explaining to us recently, you meet them in forms which call for great ingenuity, flexibility, and understanding. In such situations one must be able to distinguish between the stunt and the genuine adaptation, one must be able with intelligence and imagination to experiment in communication without jeopardizing the integrity of the Christian Faith. But since this is true in one way or another of every situation, we shall do well to know and to face our deficiencies in order to remove them.

In a recent survey of homiletical instruction in

American seminaries, Dr. Fehl has brought together in summary form an imposing body of opinion concerning these deficiencies. If they were deficiencies only in the practice-preaching of seminarists, the seminaries themselves might be expected to deal with them. But they have already escaped the immediate grasp of the seminaries because they appear to arise mainly from pre-theological education and because they are spread widely among the men already in the ministry. From what I shall quote to you from the survey, I think you will perceive that teaching techniques and skills will not go to the root of the trouble. I think you will recognize also that while the seminaries will have to bear the brunt of grappling with the situation, it has become necessary for the whole clergy to take themselves in hand to recover not merely the art of communication, but the urgent will to communicate the Word of Redemption in a manner suitable to its divine excellency.

Here, then, are the chief deficiencies noted in the survey:

A. The problems reported by speech instructors can be summarized as the absence of an interrelatedness of preacher, situation, subject, and audience. Some have observed that recent seminarists are more introverted, less sensitive to the lay and secular mind, more inhibited, and brittle. Specific deficiencies are (1) lack of feeling for an oral style; (2) inadequate organization of materials and a lack of "movement" in the development of the theme; (3) inadequate knowledge and appreciation of the arts of persuasion.

B. Most frequently noted by instructors in homiletics are (1) a lack of intellectual security and theological competence. Student-preaching gives the impression of a polemic concern in peripheral matters and an evasion of the great themes of the Gospel. . . . (2) Poverty of imagination reflecting an inadequate background in literature, history, and the arts; (3) the need for insight into the mind of the layman and an appreciative and sympathetic understanding of the problems and needs of the secular community.

That these criticisms are believed to apply to the preaching in the average American church is evident because the survey expresses "a widespread concern over the deterioration of the American pulpit." That it does so should in itself be a matter of widespread concern. Does the nation, or even the Christian population, expect from the pulpit noble speech about great matters? We are generally thought to be glib and voluble speakers, ready at a moment's notice, at a civic dinner or at a meeting, to talk with some facility on any one of a thousand things. We are professional talkers. Sometimes I think that even our Christian propaganda appears only as an advertising campaign indistinguishable in tone and method from the others. We must not speak of God as we could speak of toothpaste, or of the Church as though it were a motor club. There is a respect that noble and competent speech receives even from those who disagree with what is being said, and from this respect they are often led to espouse what they had at first rejected. Why should people not come to church to hear great preaching? They always have, and they always will, if there is great preaching to be listened to. Far from being in despair of this, I am persuaded that we are on the threshold of a great revival of Christian preaching. But there must be a recovery of nerve, of confidence in preaching. In order to preach you have to believe in it.

And now that your courtesy has followed me to the end of these lectures, be patient yet for a moment to hear my apologia for what I have said.

I do not deceive myself into supposing that I have taught you how to preach or to make a sermon, for this, with much more besides, belongs to the class-room. Although I have been speaking of Christian eloquence, I have spoken rather of the need for it and the exaltation of it than of any method of acquiring it. Until a man has a consuming desire to preach the Gospel, and until he realizes that preaching is a colloquy even though the person spoken to is not answering audibly, you cannot teach him how to preach any more than you can teach someone to play the piano who cares nothing for music. To desire to preach the Gospel with power, that is the main thing. This is why I have been playing to you a theme and variations whose melody is the excellency of the Divine Word. I have no other purpose than this, no thesis to argue, no technique to expound, no brave new method to purvey.

I have had much to say about the Holy Trinity because it is the Christian doctrine of God, the inevitable picture cast glowingly upon the human mind, as the Church believes, by the shining mystery of Jesus. For this, as the ground for considering the meaning of the Christian life, I think I have high authority. In the Epistle to the Ephesians, St. Paul summons an august body of doctrine, beginning with the lofty introduction in which he moves, as the Creed does, from the Father, to the Son, to the Holy Spirit, to the Church, as the ground for exhortation to the simplest domestic virtues. Surely there is no other ground for meditating on the work of the Christian ministry.

I have asked you to view the ministry of the Word as inseparable from priesthood because the Word of Oblation, in the liturgy, in the liturgical year, and the liturgical life, is the expression of the Christian *Koinonia*. There is a mystery of power to lead captivity captive by releasing men and women from the frustration of the secular order.

And so, finally, I believe that everything depends on our seeing, on our deeply feeling with wonder and admiration, that our ministry is for the distribution of Christ, as Bread and as Word, so that we enter the pulpit with the same solemn direction of intention with which we approach the altar. In every act of ministering, whether of word or of work, we are ascending to the altar, not alone, but with our brethren in Christ. If while you are here, we can help you to see this and to desire it, there is no greater thing we can do for you.

Appendix

A SURVEY OF
HOMILETICS EDUCATION
By

Noah E. Fehl

I

THE PROBLEMS

DURING the past three years a half dozen questionnaires have been circulated among theological schools on the personnel, curriculum, and projected changes in the teaching of homiletics. In 1953 a special gift from Mr. Charles Ward Seabury for the strengthening of our own Homiletics Department led us to solicit the counsel of our colleagues in other seminaries. The following letter was accordingly sent to thirty-six professors in leading and representative divinity schools:

> It would be helpful to us to know (1) what courses are now being offered in your depart-

ment; (2) your conclusions as to the areas of instruction most needed by seminarians in their preparation for effective preaching; (3) your evaluation of the importance of courses in style and composition, public speaking, the techniques of discussion and persuasion, literature and literary criticism, types of sermons (expository, liturgical, special occasions, etc.); (4) what program of practice preaching you have found to yield the best results in motivation and learning.

Primarily we want to know where you think the center of gravity ought to be in an effective homiletics program today and what methods of instruction and training have, in your experience, yielded the best results.

The prompt and full response to these enquiries reflects the gravity of pressures under which we are endeavoring to prepare men for the preaching ministry.[1] The common note in all this correspondence is the sober recognition of a waning both in power and influence of the American pulpit. There is also a significant area of agreement regarding the factors both within the seminaries and outside them which

[1] In reply to our survey we received in addition to departmental literature twenty-three personal letters averaging over two typewritten pages in length. These included reports from the representative schools of the seven major Protestant Communions.

may be contributing to inadequate preparation for the preaching ministry.

Implicit in all recent studies [2] and explicit in many of the replies to our enquiry is the observation that a rethinking of the task of the Homiletics Department points up a needed rethinking of aims, curriculum, and methods of theological education in general. For the most part the modern seminary curriculum continues to presuppose a background and preparation in pre-theological studies that, though still recommended, has long ceased to be the expected standard. The following summary of replies compares the standards expected a generation ago which are merely ideal today with the patterns of preparation now widely accepted.

A. Presupposed:

    1. A church family background with normal Christian nurture in the home and community, providing an intimate knowledge of the

[2] In addition to our own enquiry we have profited from (1) a reading of returns from 88 colleges and 23 seminaries on a survey of pre-theological and seminary courses in speech and homiletics and an inventory of present problems and needs conducted by the National Association of Speech Teachers, and (2) the research data compiled by Dr. Charles A. McGlon for his doctoral dissertation on *A History of Speech Education and Homiletics in American Seminaries from 1819 to 1948.*

Bible and some acquaintance with the later classics of Christian thought and devotion.

2. A record of scholastic distinction in high school and college.

3. College majors in the humanities, philosophy, and history, with a foundation in the classical languages and literatures.

4. Special talent already well developed in speaking, writing, and reading abilities and in social arts and skills.

B. Actual:

1. A substantial proportion of men in seminary have come to their sense of vocation only two years prior to graduation from college, were previously nominal Christians, and were raised in a predominantly secular environment. They have only a limited knowledge of the Bible, Christian classics, parish life, and the interests, attainments, and point of view of laymen.

2. An increasing number of applicants for seminary instruction rank in the middle or lower third of their college classes. Few have profited from the older tradition in clerical homes and in the parish community of broad and godly learning.

3. Many students admitted to seminary instruc-

tion have college majors in physical sciences, business administration, and technical arts.

4. Many students are deficient in English composition and in writing and reading abilities as well as the wider background that special competence in these areas implies.

The second factor widely recognized as basic in the rethinking of aims and methods in homiletics instruction today is the change in the status and role of the minister in the community from that of intellectual arbiter and seer in the colonial period to that of representative of one institution or agency among many in the modern urban community.

A third factor, emphasized by some, is the effect upon ministerial students of difficulties inherent in their interpretation of vocation, motivation for study, and the fulfillment of their ministry in an age characterized by transition and revolution in the theological disciplines. Unable to accept the demands of the "insistent present" as challenge and opportunity, many young men are coming to seminary to escape the problems of secular life and, in the cozy confines of a contemplative or priestly ministry, to evade fundamental theological issues to which even the secular world is sensitive and, in a measure, committed.

The problems reported by speech instructors can be summarized as the absence of an interrelatedness of preacher, situation, subject, and audience. Some have observed that recent seminarists are more introverted, less sensitive to the lay and secular mind, more inhibited, and brittle. Specific deficiencies are (1) lack of feeling for an oral style; (2) inadequate organization of materials and a lack of "movement" in the development of the theme; (3) inadequate knowledge and appreciation of the arts of persuasion.

Most frequently noted by instructors in homiletics are (1) a lack of intellectual security and theological competence. Student preaching gives the impression of a polemic concern in peripheral matters and an evasion of the great themes of the Gospel. We must remark a strange new fear of heterodoxy in the recent seminarist. This fear is strange and new in that it seems not so much an affirmation of the power and relevance of a venerable tradition as an inhibition to prove that power and to demonstrate its adequacy. Many postulants have responded to the vocation of custodian of an ancient repository of sacred lore who have not heard the "Macedonian call." (2) Poverty of imagination reflecting an inadequate background in literature, history, and the arts; (3) the need for insight into the mind of the layman and an appreciative and sympathetic understanding of the problems and needs of the secular community.

II

SURVEY OF PRESENT STANDARDS

The standard for the seminary curriculum is now a three-course sequence in homiletics with two additional courses in public speaking and oral interpretation. An introductory course on the principles of the writing and delivery of sermons is followed by one of a variety of courses on types of sermons (expository, topical, special occasions, liturgical, etc.). The third course is clinical with the emphasis upon practice preaching and individual conferences. Some seminaries require as many as twelve semester hours in homiletics including courses in the preaching values of the Old and New Testaments, Christian classics, modern literature, persuasion, history of preaching, reading and analysis of the essay form, and leadership in discussion. Many Roman Catholic seminaries have recently introduced required courses in persuasion and discussion.

For Episcopal seminaries the standard requirement in homiletics is six semester hours divided into six one-hour, two three-hour, or three two-hour courses. One school finds the one-hour course preferable for the reason that the student's attention is directed to the preaching values of all his content courses and is throughout his seminary career under the discipline of the writing of sermons. Other schools are favorably disposed to the more intensive training of the two- or three-course sequence. Two seminaries subject their seniors to a rigorous examination of proficiency in composition and the integrity of theme development. Several require extensive reading in theology, literature, and exegetical studies in conjunction with a specific practice preaching assignment. One seminary supplies reading lists of books in theology, poetry, the modern novel, and drama, with suggested texts and topics to be exploited in connection with the practical training appointments of the Trinity Term.

III

RECOMMENDATIONS

Projected plans and recommendations toward an adequate homiletics program as indicated in the replies to our survey can be summarized under six headings:

1. Seminaries must meet and not simply compromise with the deficiencies of entering students. Courses in literature with particular attention to the essay form and oral style (rhetoric) are being taught in a number of schools and listed as projected courses by others. One school has recently instituted a required three-course sequence in "Christianity and the Arts." Another plans to adopt an "orientation" prerequisite to homiletics courses which will be based upon a reading course in the essay form and a class in English composition. It is further recommended that literary and discussion societies be revived in both colleges and seminaries.

2. There is a trend toward making courses in practice preaching and tutorial sessions the center of gravity in the homiletics program.

3. Both in the pulpit and for the opportunities

of witness in the secular community a greater knowledge and use of the arts of persuasion and discussion are demanded of the modern minister. The parish minister is no longer the intellectual arbiter in his community. He is less frequently invited to lecture and preach at community functions than to represent the Church or his parish as one institution among the many civic and cultural agencies of the city. These occasions call for special skills in panel discussions and social leadership. Some schools have already provided courses in persuasion and discussion. Others are revising present courses to include instruction in these skills.

4. Several instructors advocate an achievement examination in preaching and oral interpretation requiring a minimum standard of proficiency for graduation.

5. In churches where the sacramental ministry is emphasized there is a need to exalt the place of preaching in the liturgy and to counsel a sound and wholesome insistence upon the Word *and* the Sacraments in the rationale of the total curriculum as a training for the priesthood. Where the departments of liturgics and homiletics are unrelated the student

is invited to make a choice! There is, at least on the part of the homiletics instructors, an awareness of the failure of our seminaries to impress our future clergy with the fact that an essential part of our liturgy is the preaching of the Word.

6. The greatest need appears to be a more definite interrelatedness of the speech and homiletics departments with those of Bible and theology. Most instructors feel that what were designed as helpful distinctions in the curriculum between the content courses and the practical field have become hurtful divisions. Bible and theology must be instructionally related to homiletics. Students cannot and ought not to be expected to make the transition themselves from higher criticism and a formal treatment of Biblical and theological concepts to the preaching of the Word. Greater emphasis in the content courses should be given to the seminal ideas of the Judaeo-Christian perspective. Bible and theology and Church history must be studied existentially in the content courses if they are to be effectively appropriated in homiletics.

It is further suggested that the homiletics instructor should be above all a well-rounded man, an experienced teacher, and one who has broad academic interests with special competence in Bible and theology. An adequate homiletics program cannot be administered by a one-man department. Ideally the whole faculty should be directly involved in the teaching of homiletics. A close association including the exchange of personnel should be developed among the departments of Bible, theology, and homiletics.